Thriving in a Multi-generational Law Firm

How to Increase Communication and Collaboration Among Lawyers

Authors
Pamela DeNeuve and John Grimley

Managing director
Sian O'Neill

Thriving in a Multi-generational Law Firm: How to Increase Communication and Collaboration Among Lawyers **is published by**

Globe Law and Business Ltd
3 Mylor Close
Horsell
Woking
Surrey GU21 4DD
United Kingdom
Tel: +44 20 3745 4770
www.globelawandbusiness.com

Printed and bound by Severn, Gloucester, UK

Thriving in a Multi-generational Law Firm: How to Increase Communication and Collaboration Among Lawyers

ISBN 9781787425101
EPUB ISBN 9781787425118
Adobe PDF ISBN 9781787425125

Table of contents

I. Introduction

1. Challenges in communication

In all parts of the world, multi-generational law firms face challenges in terms of communication within the firm, in particular in these areas:

- different ways of communicating;
- use of technology;
- work ethic;
- turnover;
- rising costs of attrition;
- frustration between generations;
- disharmony and low morale;
- difficulty retaining women and minority lawyers; and
- threats to profitability.

1.1 Different ways of communicating

In this Special Report we will compare three generations:

- grandfather;
- son/daughter; and
- grandchild.

In any field, if these three generations worked on a project they would each have a different approach. Essentially, the syndrome is the same for a law firm – and the age differences are wide.

1.2 Use of technology

The legal sector has historically been slow to adopt technology innovations,[1] while in general younger generations began using technology early, in some cases from as young as three. This reluctance is the result of a combination of the partnership model, the profession's risk aversion and the billable-hour business model. Work often involves slow and meticulous sifting of precedent, with minimal time focused on the exploration of new technologies.

Now, however, the expectations of clients are changing while at the same time the use of technology in the law is increasing. In addition, new entrants to the legal services market are successfully fusing legal services and technology to provide cost-efficient and more satisfying customer experiences.

1.3 Work ethic

It is not unreasonable to suggest that an individual's background might affect their work ethic. For example, younger generations began using technology early, in some cases from as young as three. Technology made everything easy. Compare this with more senior lawyers who adopted computer and internet use when they were 30, 40 or even 50 years old.

1.4 Turnover

Leaving a law firm role is often a straightforward decision for many younger lawyers. If you are unhappy or feel like the job is a dead end, it is time to leave and find greener pastures. Senior lawyers complain that they had no idea when young lawyers or staff members were unhappy. Millennials and Generation X often wonder why law firm leaders take their departures personally.

1.5 Rising costs of attrition

A recent study of 800 law firms found that for every 20 associates hired, 15 left. The average rate of associate attrition between 2012 and 2018 was 18%.[2]

More than ever before, younger associates are willing to leave a firm within the first few years. As of 2016, the top 400 law firms in the US were losing approximately $9.1 billion per year as a result of turnover, and this figure will undoubtedly have increased.[3] And this loss of lawyers, where numerous hours of training are wasted, contributes to low morale, disrupts firm cultures, damages firm reputations and is disturbing to clients.

1.6 Frustration between generations

For the first time in history, four generations are currently working together in the workforce – the silent generation, baby boomers,

"The generational shift occurring in law firms presents an opportunity for lawyers to seek to understand the generations and take steps to create custom business approaches for each."

Gen X and millennials. And each of these generations have their own distinct preferences, values and traits. The generational shift occurring in law firms presents an opportunity for lawyers to seek to understand the generations and take steps to create custom business approaches for each. Where firms do not adapt, generational friction, turnover and client loss are likely to continue.

In addition, law firms are failing to transition their leadership, business and relationship opportunities quickly enough, particularly from boomers to Gen Xers.[4]

It is critical that law firms who want to succeed adopt new styles of communication, help foster alternative career tracks and expand programmes aimed at mentoring.

1.7 Disharmony and low morale in the firm

Communication is essential for law firms to operate effectively. Without it, disharmony results. This book will explore ways to improve harmony and efficiency.

Frequent departures by law firm partners are a sign of disharmony. Firms that perform well maintain harmony between partners, associates and staff. They share a common vision. With internal conflict comes stress. The legal profession is a high-pressure environment for many, involving long hours which have a detrimental effect on mental health and morale.

1.8 Difficulty retaining women and minority lawyers

Advancement of minority lawyers has been sluggish. Over the past decade, the average growth in numbers across law firms has been 0.9% per year; and the number of minority attorneys in America's largest law firms over the same period has increased by a mere 3.9%.[5]

Moreover, a recent American Bar Association (ABA) study reports that women of colour represent approximately 2% of all equity partners at large law firms.[6] And while women make up 45–50% of law school graduates (and have done for years), they account, according to a 2019 ABA report, for 20% of equity partners and less than 25% of law firm management, practice group leaders and office leaders.[7]

According to the ABA, 85% of US-based minority female lawyers will leave large firms within seven years of beginning practice, not because they desire to leave or are unable to do the work, but because they "feel they have no choice".[8]

Black attorneys are, and have historically been, markedly underrepresented in law – more so than Latino and Asian-American lawyers. Thirteen per cent of the US population overall, Black lawyers represent less than 2% of Big Law partners.[9]

1.9 Threats to profitability

The legal profession is threatened by forces outside the traditional law firm business model, including the Big 4, NewLaw and other alternative legal services providers.

Keeping pace with technology, and staff retention (sections 1.2 and 1.4 above) are two key challenges facing law firm profitability, representing the major competitive threats to the law firm business model and changing client demands and economic conditions.[10]

2. Navigating the challenges

This Special Report is intended for all lawyers – management, students, law school administrators and legal professionals – because the challenges face all organisations. We will break down each of the topics above and look at the tools necessary to overcome and thrive.

Management committees, compensation committees and human resources will also find this Special Report of interest as they seek to examine and reassess policies and procedures that may unintentionally have led to a non-progressive and non-equitable culture that is strangling the profitability of their organisations.

Law students will also find it an invaluable resource as they prepare for the environments and difficulties they may face when they embark on their law careers.

Women and other minority groups will find suggestions for addressing the barriers they face and building a stronger presence and track record of success in their legal careers.

Each generation – Silent, boomers, Gen X, millennials (Gen Y) and Gen Z – should use this Special Report to help them understand other members of their firm, whether management, colleagues or team members.

Our aim is to provide a strategic outline to support better communication, productivity, harmony and profitability within the law firm community.

II. Generations within law firms

Strife between the generations can cause a stressful environment where lawyers young and old are at greater risk of illness. According to a well-known study by the American Heart Association, workers who feel unfairly criticised by a boss or that their supervisor doesn't listen to their concerns, have a 30% higher rate of coronary disease than those who feel appreciated.[11]

1. The problem with blaming others

At the root of the challenges between the generations is the notion of blaming others. Senior lawyers tend to hold younger lawyers responsible for problems including a lack of work ethic, commitment to the firm and willingness to conform. Younger lawyers, in turn, resent and may feel victimised by senior lawyers – creating a cycle of blame which sows division and silent or covert acrimony.

It's much better to approach differences between the generations from a perspective of understanding rather than blame – while some complaints may be justified, we encourage moving past blame to find solutions.

Friction might begin, for example, when impatient older law firm partners complain about the 'good old days' when lawyers "did the work and didn't complain".

"It's much better to approach differences between the generations from a perspective of understanding rather than blame – while some complaints may be justified, we encourage moving past blame to find solutions."

During questions following a speech at a Bar Association event in the Midwest on this topic, a boomer law firm partner, whom we'll call Ned, complained about his problems with millennials as if these young folks were the enemy. He spat out 'millennials' as if it were a dirty word. Clearly, until Ned changes his mindset there will be no harmony, either for him or the millennials he feels forced to hire.

On another occasion, one young woman from a panel of millennials, an associate we'll call Nancy, said: "I guess we will have to put up with the older generation until they eventually retire."

Many senior lawyers value tradition, while millennials often have a more wide-ranging set of aspirations.

Neither Ned nor Nancy displayed a desire to understand lawyers from different generations. They were fixated on who was to blame. They wanted to point the finger and recite the problems instead of seeking solutions. The only thing that results from blame is more problems, increased misunderstanding and continued divisions.

In this chapter, we look at the need to understand rather than be understood; we walk in another's shoes. For example, to solve divisions between the generations an individual must have the desire to succeed as part of a firm rather than to be 'right'.

At a local meeting for lawyers, a grey-haired man who identified himself as a litigator – let's call him Louis – said this: "We are not babysitters here. Practising law is a rough and tumble kind of profession. These lawyers need tough skin and must grow up ..."

We laughed and asked Louis to tell us how he really felt!

Thankfully, we were able to convince Louis that he and lawyers like him must seek to understand younger lawyers so that everyone can find a solution and everyone can succeed.

We do not confine this advice to senior lawyers. Younger lawyers, Gen Xers and millennials must also make the commitment to understanding senior lawyers who are their employers and colleagues.

Those lawyers, young and old, who insist on being positional and blaming others will find no peace. The attitude will cost firms millions in productivity and turnover. To succeed and thrive within a law firm, the four generations must learn to respect and understand each other, and to work together despite their differences.

2. Understanding the generations

Understanding different generational experiences will allow managers to adjust their communication and leadership styles to engage, empower and encourage all of their employees. It will help in mentoring younger lawyers, promote cooperation and create unity to solidify a law firm's future.

In the following sections we will review the background, environment and current events that distinguished each generation. This will help us to understand what moulded their respective belief systems and values.

Of course, there are always exceptions – we will be making generalisations based on our experience and research.

2.1 The silent generation (born 1925–1945)

This generation suffered many hardships – world wars, The Great Depression. Times were hard. People had to sacrifice. Family unity was strong. The belief was that everyone should earn their keep and pay their dues. Frugality was valued. Everything had to be earned by following the rules and working hard.

Table 1. Silent generation

Defining events/movements	• The Great Depression • Stock market collapse • 25% of workforce unemployed • The New Deal: relief, reform, recovery • Rise in suicide rates during Depression • World War II • Rationing of food, gas, clothing • Women hired to replace men at war • Fewer children • Korean War • 60% drop in farm prices
Characteristics	• Religious • Patriarchal • Respect authority • Follow rules and traditions • Value hard work and sacrifice • Believe in 'waste not, want not' • Are loyal to employers
Notable individuals	• Queen Elizabeth II • Robin Knox-Johnston • Margaret Thatcher • Marilyn Monroe • John Lennon • Fidel Castro • Mick Jagger

2.2 The baby boomers (born 1946–1964)

The boomers, the largest generation before millennials, are still a force to be reckoned with. They seek to stay youthful as long as possible. Many do not see retirement as desirable and want to work for as long as possible. Baby boomers value education, personal growth and personal satisfaction. They put their career as their highest priority, often before family, and can be driven and highly ambitious.

Table 2. Baby boomers

Defining events/movements	• End of World War II • Soldiers return from war • A boom of new babies born

continued on next page

Defining events/movements *(continued)*	• Civil rights movement and Dr Martin Luther King • John F Kennedy elected president and later assassinated • Cuban Missile Crisis • Vietnam War • Hippie movement • Television expansion and boom • Birth control pill introduced • Feminism and sexual revolution • Reduction in family sizes • Increase in divorce rate • Experimentation with marijuana and psychedelic drugs • Counterculture and protest • Rock n' roll, Beatles and Elvis Presley • First moon landing • AIDS epidemic
Characteristics	• Strong work ethic • Goal-oriented • 10–25 years longer life expectancy than parents • Not eager or financially able to retire • Suffer income insecurity • Challenge the status quo • Seek immediate gratification • Set out to accomplish individual goals • Have higher IQs than parents due to improved nutrition • Challenge traditional religion • Embrace the self-help movement
Notable individuals	• Princess Diana • Tom Cruise • Elton John • Oprah Winfrey • Steve Jobs • Bill Gates • Vladimir Putin • Barack Obama • Kamala Harris • Steven Spielberg • Xi Jinping • Jeff Bezos

2.3 Generation X (born 1965–1980)

Gen X became a generation of independent and critical thinkers. They did not blindly accept what the older generation considered to be right. In 2008 they witnessed their parents losing savings that they had sacrificed and worked hard for. This made these critical thinkers want to pave another path for themselves. With the computer and the dot-com bubble, many became entrepreneurs. They are not in a hurry to marry and repeat the mistakes of their parents, many of whose marriages ended in divorce.

Table 3. Generation X

Defining events/movements	• Introduction of the personal computer • Increasing divorce rates • More mothers in the workforce • Latch-key generation (less supervision) • Fall of the Berlin Wall • Challenger disaster • Energy crisis • Watergate scandal • President Nixon impeached in the US • AIDS epidemic – one to two million HIV positive • Crack epidemic and anti-drug programmes • Rodney King beating and nationwide riots • Iran hostage crisis • Stock market decline • Terrorism at the Munich Olympics • Gen Xers labelled 'Thatcher's children' in the UK
Characteristics	• Entrepreneurial spirit • Individualism • Patriotism • Familiarity with computers and devices • Excellent education • Creation of high-tech industries • Self-confidence and optimism • No hurry to grow up (as tradition dictates) • Questioning of the economy and financial institutions • Reluctance to sell out ideals • Often considered 'slackers'
Notable individuals	• JK Rowling • Sergey Brin and Larry Page (founders of Google) • Elon Musk

continued on next page

Notable individuals *(continued)*	• David Beckham • Tiger Woods • Jay Z • Susan Wojcicki (CEO of YouTube) • David Cameron • Kate Winslet • Leonardo DiCaprio • Peyton Manning

2.4 Millennials (born 1981–1996)

Millennials tend to be better educated and focus more on their family and well-being. They have brought more racial and ethnic diversity to society. Women are being recognised as never before. Millennials are poised to lead law firms throughout the world and are ready for change. They challenge the hierarchy and status quo. Their trust in governments and organisations has been eroded.

Table 4. Millennials (also known as Gen Y)

Defining events/movements	• 9/11 terrorist attacks • Wars in Iraq and Afghanistan • Intense political polarisation • The first black US president • 2008 economic recession • Explosion of the internet and information age • Introduction of the iPod and the smartphone • Apple and the democratisation of music • Social media platforms: Facebook, Twitter, Instagram, YouTube • Increase in gun violence in schools • Death of Princess Diana • Murder of Treyvon Martin triggering Black Lives Matter (BLM) movement • COVID-19 pandemic • Same-sex marriage largely recognised
Characteristics	• Digital natives • Lives defined by the internet • Heavy social media users • Smartphone users • Consumers of digital music • Largely users of YouTube • Consider Google a necessity

continued on next page

Characteristics *(continued)*	• Two out of three males play video games regularly • Diversity is a way of life • Most are highly educated • Question all traditions • Culturally diverse • Burdened with large education debts • Large percentage still live at home • Leave jobs frequently seeking better opportunities • Live in shared spaces • In no hurry to get married • Deeply impacted by the 2008 economic recession • Deeply impacted by the COVID-19 pandemic
Notable individuals	• Prince William • Joshua Wong • Olivia Wilde • Alexandria Ocasio-Cortez • Andy Murray • Tom Holland • LeBron James • Adele • Mark Zuckerberg • Justin Bieber • Kendrick Lamar • Lady Gaga • Serena Williams

2.5 Generation Z (born 1997–2015)

Gen Z can be hard workers. As many Gen Zers are still minors, they tend to protest on social media rather than in person. They want their voices heard and they are learning from the previous generation's mistakes. All indicators suggest that this generation are engaged, conscientious stewards of our world. They are more united, socially and politically, than their predecessors. They are independent thinkers who recognise their responsibility in shaping a more equitable future for all.

Table 5. Generation Z (also known as zoomers)

Defining events/movements	• COVID-19 pandemic • Intense political polarisation • 2008 economic recession • Peak technological age • Age of the digital natives • Era of child smartphone users • Ubiquity of text messaging • Daily life defined by social media • Age of the selfie • Increased gun violence • Gender equality and fluidity • Climate change • Black Lives Matter (BLM) • Murder of George Floyd • Same-sex marriage largely recognised
Characteristics	• 73% of Gen Z have video game consoles[12] • 95% of 13–17-year-olds have smartphones[13] • 97% use at least one major online platform[14] • Widespread usage of portable digital technology at a young age • Advanced digital sophistication • Belief in action rather than words • Can be characterised as 'always-on' • Conscious and caring about the planet and its people • Stereotyped as tech-addicted, social justice warriors • Politically progressive • Believe in shared family responsibilities • Enjoy continually sharing experiences

continued on next page

Notable individuals	<ul><li>Greta Thunberg</li><li>Billie Eilish</li><li>Amika George</li><li>Simone Biles</li><li>Naomi Osaka</li><li>Malala Yousafzai</li><li>Amanda Gorman</li><li>Hadiqa Bashir</li><li>Elle van der Burg</li><li>Rowan Blanchard</li><li>Amandla Stenberg</li></ul>

3. Summary

While holding others to account may be justified, we believe it is important to move past blame and to find solutions that are sensitive to the background and history of each generation. The social, financial and historical environment has much to do with each generation's values. We must use this information to move away from finding fault, as the alternative is stagnation.

Effective communication is the only way lawyers can bridge the gap between the generations. It is the best way to facilitate an interchange of thoughts, opinions and information. In the next chapter we will consider the mindsets that help us to adopt best practice in inter-generational communication.

III. Inter-generational communication

1. Introduction

Often, the culture of law firms actually creates inter-generational friction.

Case study

'Susan'[15] worked at an elite American Big Law firm. She paid her dues in an elite law school and in her first few years in her firm. However, she witnessed a recurring situation in the firm that she found troubling. Sometimes, ambitious young junior lawyers tried to position themselves favourably *vis-à-vis* other associates. A culture of ambition helped create a highly competitive climate among junior lawyers, which sometimes manifested itself in selfish and destructive behaviours. More cooperative junior lawyers like Susan were sidelined in favour of more aggressively competitive ones, and eventually she moved on.

When law firms promote a ruthless and competitive culture it results in the loss of morale – and good lawyers.

2. The solution begins with understanding

When lawyers belong to the same generation, they often share similar communication styles. By focusing on the differences and similarities in communication style between the generations, they can begin to understand each other, and to stop citing others as the source of the problem. This conversation is the beginning of improved communication, and mentoring and can help in this context.

Based on our review of each generation in the previous chapter, we can offer a number of suggestions for best practice in inter-generational communication. Below, we look at the respective mindsets and the best way to communicate generation by generation.

3. Better communication according to generation

3.1 The silent generation

Consider these mindsets and principles associated with the silent generation:

- personal responsibility;
- integrity;
- humility;
- work ethic;
- service;
- commitment;
- tendency not to complain;
- acceptance of authority; and
- stiff upper lip.

"Communicating with the silent generation is helped by displaying courtesy, respect, appreciation for their experience and an understanding that they have valuable knowledge that is helpful for young lawyers."

Communicating with the silent generation is helped by displaying courtesy, respect, appreciation for their experience and an understanding that they have valuable knowledge that is helpful for young lawyers. Their skills with technology may be limited, which requires patience. Allow them to tell their story, however long it may take.

3.2 Baby boomers

Consider the mindsets and principles of baby boomers:

- strong work ethic;
- independence of thought;
- competitive spirit;
- goals orientation;
- discipline;
- mental focus;
- wish to stay young;
- money focus;
- tendency towards materialism; and
- willingness to put career first.

Boomers appreciate being given growth opportunities to succeed within their organisations. They appreciate working with others who also have ambition. They also value personal growth, teamwork and personal satisfaction, often seeing themselves as central to their work community. It helps to provide them with an opportunity to be organisational stars.

3.3 Gen X

Consider the mindsets and principles of Gen X:

- independence/self-sufficiency;
- ability to adapt to social change and upheaval;
- tendency towards critical thinking;
- individualism;
- willingness to question traditional ways of thinking;
- suspicion of financial structures;
- reliance on computers and other devices;
- awareness of diversity and equality;
- good education;
- orientation towards family;
- tendency to be single longer before marriage;
- resourcefulness;
- appreciation of freedom and responsibility; and
- inclination to address challenges independently.

Let Gen X know that work/life balance is important and emphasise the necessity of technology with opportunities for remote working and

"Examining the mindsets of the different generations facilitates the elimination of friction in communication between them. It means we can stop citing other generations as the source of the problem."

independent thinking. Allowing them to be individualistic, self-motivated and resourceful will be appreciated.

3.4 Millennials

Consider the mindsets and principles of millennials:

- confidence;
- self-reliance;
- dependence on technology;
- tendency to be socially outgoing;
- susceptibility to depression;
- image awareness;
- achievement orientation;
- communication skill;
- willingness to question authority;
- desire to search out new challenges;
- unwillingness to trust governments and organisations;
- desire to find work/life balance;
- readiness to ask why;
- acceptance of mentoring & desire to learn;
- appreciation of regular feedback;
- need for meaningful motivation;
- willingness to challenge the hierarchy status quo;
- tendency to place importance on relationships with superiors;
- possession of an intuitive knowledge of technology;
- readiness to adapt to change; and
- tendency to place importance on tasks rather than time.

Millennials do not like limitations.

Many activities are conducted online, on smartphones. Millennials are more open to diversity than their seniors. They spend more time with their children than previous generations, especially fathers.

Money is not the primary incentive for millennials; instead they prefer law firms that provide personal growth, challenges and opportunity for teamwork. Partners will want to be coaches more than bosses, emphasising teamwork and frequent interaction.

3.5 Gen Z

Consider the mindsets and principles of Gen Z. They tend to:

- see caring about other groups as a core value;
- be better educated;
- base a big part of their lives on the gaming community;
- embrace formal volunteering;
- care deeply about full equality;

- depend on devices, internet and social media;
- suffer from sleep deprivation;
- be more risk-averse; and
- suffer from mental health issues.

Gen Zers, like millennials, have been raised to be independent and figure things out for themselves, needing less positive reinforcement.

Gen Z represent the leading edge of society's changing racial and ethnic makeup. They are more diverse. They are native to technology and have much to contribute to law firms.

4. Summary

Examining the mindsets of the different generations facilitates the elimination of friction in communication between them. It means we can stop citing other generations as the source of the problem.

Building on the foundation of understanding, we can begin to open the door to better unity and communication among lawyers. In the chapters that follow, we will look at survey responses from practising lawyers that reveal the problems many experience, and how they deal with them.

IV. Survey of lawyers

1. Introduction

We wanted to take the opportunity, using polls, questionnaires and interviews – with lawyers from various generations – to get a sense of their differing views and the obstacles they face. Many of our respondents were members of LinkedIn, the pre-eminent social media platform for professionals, with millions of users (at the time of writing, over 770 million users in more than 200 countries).[16]

Lawyers are heavy users of LinkedIn, where they seek employment, networking opportunities and strengthening of professional relationships.

We created a random poll, asking lawyers who use the platform to tell us which generation they represented, and to answer the same five questions. The poll was viewed over 8,000 times and received 238 responses. Table 6 shows the percentage of respondents from the various generations.

Table 6. Respondents by generation

Generation	Response rate
Silent generation	0%
Baby boomers	11%
Generation X	28%
Millennials (Generation Y)	61%
Generation Z (zoomers)	0%

We are not suggesting that these figures represent hard and fast data – most of the silent generation are now retired or deceased, boomers are not the majority on social media, and Gen Z (the oldest of whom are still in their early twenties) have not yet signed up to LinkedIn in great numbers. Gen X and millennials, however, have a strong presence on the platform, together making up 89% of respondents.

Those surveyed, therefore, can be said to represent a microcosm of the outside world but with caveats. Boomers, for example, might feel that personal and business success, often achieved through in-person interaction, owes little to a specific social media platform. To be a proficient thought leader on LinkedIn requires application, and many boomers might not see the value of investing time and money to enhance their LinkedIn brand.

2. Five questions about generational differences

We posed five questions to lawyers in the different generations, which will be discussed in turn in the sections that follow:

1. ***What are the biggest challenges you experience when communicating with other generations?***

2. ***What are the challenges affecting your work and productivity?***

3. ***What would make it easier to work with other generations?***

4. ***What would you change?***

5. ***How are you willing to change to improve communication, work and productivity?***

Q 1: What are the biggest challenges you experience when communicating with other generations?

Millennials should focus on the job: One boomer respondent told us that many times she did not want to talk about things and didn't want to thrash things out. She did not care about feelings. It seemed to her that millennials shouldn't care about how they feel and instead should focus on getting the job done.

Boomers could be "more polite": One millennial said he sees effective communication – particularly when asking for help – as something that can be done politely and in person, and not by barking orders via email. He feels that emails come across as cold and demanding.

Boomers are reluctant to use technology: In another case, a millennial told us that he sees a way in which work – and favours – can be more effectively communicated. He said that he comes "from a communication age", and that boomers have a reluctance to use technology, which ultimately impedes smooth communication between the generations.

Older lawyers are reluctant to see things in a new way: A millennial with almost ten years' experience sees older lawyers as stuck in their ways. She believes that older lawyers don't care how millennials feel, but rather about how the millennials that they supervise do their job. She sees a disconnect with the human aspect. It's more in tone than anything. This causes her to retreat and struggle to actually get the work done. It therefore serves to demotivate her and causes many other problems. She's disillusioned when boomers tell her to "suck it up" and "get it done".

Millennials "need their self-worth affirmed": A boomer told us she "doesn't have problems with Gen X", but observed that:

> *The main difference is with millennials who expect me to affirm their self-worth before I give them any instructions or suggestions for improvement. They will take constructive advice and suggestions, but I have to give them a lot of affirmations in advance. I have to say I'm always walking on eggshells when I'm with them. I see Gen Z as having a totalitarian attitude and constantly disagreeing. They act as if anyone who disagrees is an evil person – which really has me walking on eggshells. It is impossible for Gen Z to have any constructive discussion, much less to be tolerant of any disagreement. When I'm around them I'm living with cancel culture.*

Technology is a dividing line between the generations: A Gen X Big Law partner told us that the use of technology has been the area in which inter-generational synergy has been most challenging:

> *The truth of the matter is we are in the midst of transition between 2D lawyers (lawyers who are used to having everything on paper, eg, paper-based affidavits, paper-based evidence, etc) and 3D lawyers (lawyers who are born of the digital age, used to working with meta-data, etc). Traditional lawyers are used to doing things by their tradition, while a new generation of lawyers' advantage lies in their innovation. That said, all lawyers should be mindful that there are phases of their practice. What they criticise their superiors today for, they will themselves be held under scrutiny for in the future.*

Culture and background impact communication more than age:

> *At least in the professional context, I don't see a significant and specific generational difficulty to communication. There are some differences though (eg, younger generations being more open to using social media to communicate rather than calling or meeting face to face). I think other factors, such as culture, nationality, background etc, may impact more significantly on communication styles. However, if I had to pick one challenge with cross-generational communication, it would be preconceived notions about people from other generations. Often it is more productive to treat others as individuals rather than representatives of a particular generation.*
> (Gen X Big Law partner)

Younger lawyers are less committed to the profession: A boomer told us:

> *There is difficulty because women have to prove themselves. A male is recognised and given opportunities that women are not given. There is an assumption that women cannot do the job as well as a male. We feel overlooked and there are no opportunities for mentors, so we are always behind. Gen X and millennials, especially, do not display the level of commitment towards the legal profession. There is a movement that has moved so far away from traditional law it is hard to recognise our profession. We wonder where the professionalism has gone?*

Millennials are 'baby lawyers': A millennial, having started her career in a Big Law firm, discovered that partners assumed that because she was younger "she had no value to add in the conversation". She felt like her contributions were dismissed.

Assumptions were based on age, her non-traditional educational path into law, and the idea that first-year lawyers had nothing of value to contribute and know less, with a perspective that was not valued. She was a 'baby lawyer'.

Millennial associates are "not committed": A Gen X lawyer told us that millennials "don't know the terminology and expectations of the legal profession". She said that when she started as an associate in 1995 a much different attitude existed. "When millennial lawyers are asked today to do something, they respond differently", she told us. Millennials "are more focused on their personal view about how they should be treated". One example, she said, was when one of her millennial colleagues, an associate, was asked to prepare a brief. On the Sunday before it was due, they said they needed an extension of two days because of the need to "take care of their horse". By Monday, she told us, the associate had simply disappeared. Millennials, she said, "are not committed, don't deliver and don't think anything about deadlines".

There is a lack of person-to-person dialogue:

> *Some people in younger generations don't want to be on the phone. They want everything to be by email, or typed letters. There is no person-to-person dialogue.*
> (Boomer)

On a more positive note, one Gen X managing partner told us he doesn't have any specific challenges with communication because he makes an effort to understand the needs of each generation with whom he interacts. And a Big Law partner suggested that it helps to swim with the tide in a digital age:

> *My job allows me to work with many start-ups, mostly created by young founders. When working with them, I found myself easily directed/affected by past experience and stereotypes formed from my 20-ish years in the legal field. To put it simply, I tend to view them as ambitious but inexperienced, or even delusional, since they haven't had that many years of working experience in their pockets and their way of seeing a matter doesn't align with mine. Nevertheless, I see this more as a difficulty from my side that I need to overcome as I understand that our society evolves constantly and these young buds are the representation of a new world full of Artificial Intelligence, Crypto Currency and automated processes. As a lawyer, I understand that I have to swim with the tide if I want to work in this digital age.*

2.1 Q 1 summary

Almost all lawyers interviewed expressed frustration, blame and anger when working with other generations; but we are encouraged by a few law firm leaders who are leaning more towards trying to understand and work with the generational differences.

The biggest difficulties that lawyers cite are:

- communication styles;
- management styles;
- work ethic;
- attitudes;
- loyalty;
- equity; and
- the need for greater technological advancement in law firms.

These issues continue to cause friction.

Q 2: What are the challenges affecting your work and productivity?

One of the most important factors to law firms is productivity and profits. Many law firms are not aware of how much inter-generational friction and communication gaps thwart productivity. We asked a selection of boomers, Gen Xers and millennials to rate how their productivity is affected by these divisions within the firm.

Willingness to try: One boomer told us that he "gets discouraged when inter-generational communications aren't working" and that he's "reluctant to even bother". Negative communications reduce productivity and make him feel "frozen" – so much so that he doesn't know what to do.

Taking time to cultivate communication:

> *If the generation gap is too wide, you will find yourself speaking another language. Take language, for example. While most of us are English-proficient today, if we travel back in time, we will find it difficult to communicate with people speaking Old English (despite the fact that it is the same language). The same applies to any organisational practices. Communication therefore takes time to cultivate. You cannot expect a new staff member to simply go 'plug and play' without investing the time to establish synergy with colleagues.*
> (Gen X Big Law partner)

Setting the right tone:

> *It is more their tone than anything. I have retreated and struggled*

"One of the most important factors to law firms is productivity and profits. Many law firms are not aware of how much inter-generational friction and communication gaps thwart productivity."

to actually get the work done and so it's a demotivator. It causes so many problems when senior lawyers say, "Suck it up and get going."
(Millennial)

Shoring up millennials' self-esteem:

[It] slows me down because I have to pay a lot of attention to their self-esteem needs before getting to client needs. Once we get through the nonsense, they are creative and always very interesting. The way they look at things is helpful if you could get to that part first. This would make things faster and more efficient. In the older generation, this issue doesn't come up. Older lawyers try to be better by being smarter, more successful and winning more cases.
(Boomer – on communication with younger lawyers)

Staying open-minded:

In order to avoid this 'experience' trap, I remind myself to stay open-minded and to think outside of the box as much as possible. I have to confess that this has not been an easy task since humans are creatures of habit – we tend to have an automatic response based on past experience.

> *To fix this, when it comes down to absorbing new knowledge and structure, I tried to learn from scratch so I can understand things from their core, which will result in better judgement on topics from my end.*
> (Big Law partner)

Dealing with gender inequality and a failure to give credit: One boomer told us:

> *The differences between women and men lawyers will never be overcome by the older generation. Women lawyers like myself continue to try to be better, be smarter, more successful and win more cases.*

She sees millennials as not preparing for their cases:

> *I would like to think that they really care about their cases and I see the emotional commitment they have to their clients. Working in mediation, however, does make it much easier to close the gap.*

She told us that these challenges caused her to work harder:

> *I had to come with receipts, or other authority, or go through numerous chains of command to be able to communicate the exact thing I was saying – because they were assumed to know more ... Ideas were always presented as others' ideas ... I got used to my ideas being co-opted.*

A millennial told us that as a woman she spent a lot of time working on things like articles, where she did all of the research but in the end was no more than an asterisk and a footnote. She said: "You have to be okay when you communicate ideas that you'll never get the credit for."

Being unable to count on young lawyers:

> *In some cases, because of this lack of commitment, it causes me to be more focused on doing it myself and not wasting time trying to get help. The result is it makes my day longer. I simply can't count on younger lawyers to help me carry the load.*
> (Gen X partner)

Dealing with more adversarial millennials: A boomer lawyer told us that it hampers her having a favourable relationship connection with millennial opposing counsel, and being able to build a relationship. "Things," she said, "are more adversarial with millennial lawyers."

2.2 Q 2 summary

It is important that all generations pay attention to this diversity of subjective experience. The bottom line is that if individuals are frustrated, profitability will suffer.

Q 3: What would make it easier to work with other generations?

The purpose of this question was to explore what kind of conciliatory actions could be taken to begin to bridge the gap. These are not isolated examples – frustration affects all sizes of law firms and all generations, worldwide.

Devote time to building relationships: One lawyer told us that devoting time to building relationships works best to help generations work together:

> *Having more non-work time together to build relationships, friendships and engage in activities to get to know each other is a good way to do this, as well as structured exercises at firm meetings, social events and lunch activities, to build trust.*

Enable two-way communication:

> *Communication, like all things, takes effort from both sides. That and technology. Technology does enable streamlined communication with instant access. However, the lack of barriers (an example being the proliferation of instant messenger apps), needs to be used with care as it is likely to expose those you work with to fatigue and burn-out.*
> (Gen X Big Law partner)

Ensure good preparation:

> *Millennials often haven't prepared their cases. But I would like to think that they really care about their cases from an emotional standpoint. That they have a commitment to their clients.*
> (Boomer)

Put yourself in their shoes:

> *When life gives you lemons, make lemonade. I think it's crucial to develop a determination to put myself in an unknown environment and make the best out of it. In addition, putting myself in their shoes and speaking in their social language has proven effective in working with younger generations. For example, they tend to be in awe when we discuss trends on TikTok that are work-related.*
> (Big Law partner)

Encourage millennials to give the job time:

> *More than open dialogue, I think we need to have difficult conversations about what both sides are expecting. The issues are twofold: as young attorneys you are very afraid of getting fired. It doesn't look good to get fired or have school debt. As Millennials we see that if it is not going to work and we are not seeing progress – it is better to leave. It's also tough if we don't get experience, particularly within our first year of employment. I myself left private practice and went into the public sector because I wasn't able to meet the billable hours requirements. I felt like I was dying at my desk and as a result I was very eager to go to the public sector. In addition, I see criminal law practice as definitely more difficult than civil law. Interviews are also a challenge as we are trying to give a good impression. Being new to a legal job has its challenges. We're often asked to make a two-year commitment. But Millennials are always moving. So, asking us to stick it out for a year or two is a challenge – as some Millennials are willing to jump if the job isn't a good fit.*
> (Millennial)

Find self-esteem in personal life, not at work: A boomer told us:

> *With Gen Z we need a commitment to free speech and frank discussion – and we need to expect a good faith attitude that when people disagree, we can still successfully move things along.*

Another boomer said:

> *Millennials should not expect their co-workers to build their self-esteem – they should find that in their personal life.*

Put women lawyers on an equal footing to men: One boomer said it would be easier if "older generations put women lawyers on equal footing with their male counterparts", creating more opportunities for mentoring.

Provide access to groups of successful women:

> *Throughout my career I was frequently the only woman lawyer. I often didn't go on business trips for critical cases. They wouldn't take me to hearings or depositions because I'm a woman. But eventually I broke the barrier and was allowed to travel. I'd previously not been included as a woman because people felt uncomfortable traveling with me. I was excluded from a hunting trip and golf – where the equipment cost $10,000. No one ever said I should join these social groups. Most participation in these*

groups was casual – making the growth of my law practice very difficult as I did not have access to the information I needed. If I'd had access to a group of successful women, I would not have had a situation where I had no access, and years went by and I missed the boat.
(Boomer)

Listen to other perspectives:

It's important for lawyers from various generations to have a willingness to at least hear another perspective. It all comes down to communication and trust. There should be a willingness to hear from and appreciate those of different ages and diversity, about people bringing gifts from different orientations – who can all listen to others from diverse backgrounds, and different generations.
(Millennial)

Lay down the law:

Firms and other organisations should seek to be clear about what their expectations are for their lawyers. There are currently no repercussions for poor performance and firms need to be much more clear about what their expectations are. If a lawyer is having a problem completing their work, either tell them you can't do it or agree on a modified work schedule. Law firms are in a quandary with how to manage their lawyers. They are making allowances, but the lawyers are paid well and must be managed from the top down. If you don't perform as a lawyer, this should show up in your salary. I do believe firms need to lay down the law.
(Gen X lawyer)

Commit to free speech and frank discussion:

I don't think there's a problem. Less trust does exist, but I like to view myself as a problem solver. Some younger lawyers are just about having a fight. Younger lawyers have a problem with their work ethic, creating a situation where cases drag out and clients end up paying a lot more money. With Gen Z a commitment to free speech and frank discussion will mean we can work in a context of good faith – when people disagree, things can still move along well.
(Boomer)

2.3 Q 3 summary

Although the purpose of this question was to look for a solution, by and large the individuals interviewed kept reverting back to the problem. It is obvious that intervention is needed because current law firm culture does not provide the tools to solve these generational differences.

Q 4: What would you change?

When we asked this question, we were looking for what individual lawyers were willing to change in their own behaviour to move closer to a solution, and what changes they would like to see in others, and in their working environment. From the responses thus far, the impression is that lawyers are stuck within the problem. They point to everything from work and technology to health, well-being, interpersonal relations, communication and engagement.

Eliminate judgement: A millennial lawyer said we need to eliminate judgement. "Older lawyers," they said, "should not judge us."

Use technology to free lawyers from excessive manual labour:

> *The biggest threats to any organisation (both law firms and elsewhere) are barriers. In a society which over-emphasises seniority over competence, it really does put up unnecessary barriers. Also, the legal profession, quite sadly to say, places an over-emphasis on manual labour (which gives rise to human errors). I would say that law firms (and the Law Society ought to take a lead role) should encourage and facilitate firms to adopt tested and approved technology. Take accounting software, for example: many law firm interventions began with violation of accounting rules (both as a result of intentional violation and inadvertence). The Law Society can take a more active role in selecting approved (and quality) accounting software and push for members' adoption. Not only will this enable uniform practice, but also reduce the need for disciplinary action (which no one wants – for all parties involved).*
> (Big Law Gen X partner)

Know how the system works:

> *Since most of the start-ups I work with are tech ones, I think it is very important to understand the technology industry besides mastering the global legal framework built for it. As a lawyer, you may not care about, for example, how Bitcoin is coded but at a minimum, you definitely need to know how the Blockchain system works and apply it to your legal work.*
> (Big Law partner)

Focus more, as a profession, on mental health:

> *The profession should change the way we approach difficult conversations and mental health, depression and anxiety – which can hit hard and makes us afraid to talk about how we feel. They say nice people won't survive it, having a difficult conversation. Let's be each other's cheerleaders. Baby Boomers and the Silent Generation will not discuss mental health, however. We should be able to talk about being overwhelmed. We all have the goal of being the best we can be, it is a measure of one's worth. The ultimate test is – make the grade – irrespective of how we feel. We are not talking about mental health, the fate of millennials, transgender rights, preferred pronouns – and we should be. It's still very much a boys' club.*
> (Millennial)

Change the expectations of millennials – life is tough:

> *I would educate the parents of Millennials – as the challenges go back to the parents – who were too concerned about keeping Millennials safe than adjusting to the reality that life is tough. Millennials should not expect everyone to treat them as carefully as their parents did – who taught them their feelings are more important than frank discussion. I've been more socially active and networked as a lawyer – and made this a huge part of my practice. I would have made some different choices when I first practiced law and would have moved on from firms that weren't working. I picked a law firm just out of law school which had 22 people. In two years, the firm quadrupled to 100 and became a very hostile environment. There, a guy asked me out and things descended pretty quickly. In retrospect, I would not have picked this firm. I should have moved on years before as soon as I became a partner. If I'd had the right mentor I would not have stayed so long. I would have known the right directions to take. I developed a sickness of spirit – but I didn't start off that way. In the beginning I had a lot of excitement and enthusiasm – but things changed enormously.*
> (Boomer)

Don't see millennials as entitled:

> *There's a lot of tension between generations. Everyone is either talking about how terrible Millennials are – or that we are entitled and want all of these things and that if we don't get them we'll leave. The philosophy in the legal profession is that you must pay your dues. During the Great Recession the legal market saw tremendous upheaval – and the parents of Millennials and others*

> *in their generation who had dedicated their lives to their careers – saw what they had worked so hard for – vanish.*
>
> *Millennials had a different experience with BigLaw as we entered knowing everyone can't become a partner, and that we would be expected to work 24 hours without caring, and that we should follow a path where we showed loyalty to an often-flawed organisation. Firms should recognise our experience is different and remove the animosity between the generations with a culture more open to listening.*
> (Millennial)

Accept that not all are up to the task: A Gen X lawyer told us that both law firm and in-house roles should make clear what the expectations are. "Some," they said, "will be up to the task and some will not."

Find favourable solutions for all:

> *Be a more cooperative, mutual advocate for clients and find a solution that favours everyone.*
> (Boomer)

Engage more: A Gen X managing partner told us he "wants to be more inclusive by engaging more".

2.4 Q 4 summary

This question – What would you change? – allowed for possible solutions to be proposed. It is encouraging that many lawyers are willing to look deeper rather than point the finger.

Q 5: How are you willing to change to improve communication, work and productivity?

This final question asked lawyers to look at how they might improve communication to increase their productivity, and to reflect on how they could change individually to bridge the communication gap.

It is clear from the responses that more training is required, as well as a greater emphasis on emotional intelligence. This will be discussed at length in a later chapter.

Adopt a risk-tolerant mindset: A boomer partner told us he's "willing to take risks and have conversations that are necessary".

Embrace the idea of a legal services technology revolution:

> *I have always been a champion for adoption of technology in our*

legal practices. Our profession is far too 2D and in the age of technology (when so much evidence and materials that we handle are digital), it is time for the entire industry to have a technological revolution. As mentioned above, the adoption of technology will both improve communication (the common tongue of the modern age) and improve productivity and efficiency.
(Big Law Gen X partner)

Foster a more cooperative work environment: A boomer told us that she wants to have "a more cooperative work environment and be an advocate for clients to find mutually effective solutions for all involved".

Be more open and honest about yourself:

I'm being more open and honest about who I am. I used to make a lot of promises and I am going to give it my best effort and express who I am. I'm asking more questions so I can make my best efforts. Seeking help when needed even when you are afraid of your boss – who seems too incredibly busy for me. I can ask my boss a question, even though he is short tempered and not going to have time to answer. I'm willing to be a little less left brain to be more empathetic to notice feelings more often than I do because that's not how I was trained. You can't expect them to be completely like you and understand that they come from a different generation.
(Millennial)

Be aware that boomer lawyers care: A boomer told us that he cares about the younger generation and is open to being helpful. Younger lawyers should be aware of this and be open to this caring.

I expected to be a partner – but the tipping point was when they began stretching the partnership process to 5, 6 and 7 years – or never – which is unworkable and selfish on the part of the firm ... I received none of the benefits of being a Boomer lawyer.

Overcome reticence about technology:

We have to be willing to be patient – like trying to get the client to go from in-person meetings to Zoom meetings – and I'm impatient about their fear and reticence of using technology. Change is uncomfortable and trying to change dramatically is even more uncomfortable. Boomers need more patience about doing things differently – as well as have more patience with us Millennials.
(Millennial)

Communicate from the client's perspective: A Gen X lawyer told us that she engages in conversations at a firm level, providing presentations and getting things done – not just saying it has to be done.

> *I'd stay up all night and do everything. Communicating from the client's perspective and what they need because they are the ones paying. If we don't do this for the client, it could lead to delays where our clients don't get their needs met.*

Exercise more patience: A boomer says she now sees more opportunities "to build productive relations between the generations", adding: "I communicate with each individual from a perspective that they prefer. I exercise more patience."

Prioritise communication: A Gen X managing partner told us that improving communication is his top priority.

2.5 Q 5 summary

Although this question, where we asked what lawyers were willing to change, opened a dialogue, with each generation looking at what they could to do to lessen friction, there still seems to be an element of blame in some of the responses.

3. Summary

It's worth taking a moment to reflect on these questions and responses – whether they seem politically correct or not. We all have biases based on our generation, background or environment. In order to resolve disparities and avoid disputes, we must be honest with ourselves, just as our respondents were. Solutions-based conversations and coaching can only come when we acknowledge our own biases and shortcomings.

Our survey revealed many differing perspectives, from all generations. In the next chapter we look at just one perspective – that of a managing partner – and offer a roadmap to resolving communication problems.

V. A managing partner's perspective

1. Introduction

Inter-generational tension in some firms is hidden beneath the surface, consigned to quiet conversations between senior lawyers as they shake their heads in disgust, or to tirades behind closed doors in the partners' meeting.

In contrast, younger lawyers complain about their difficulties with the firm, and the partners, over lunch. These lunchtime discussions may be the launch pad from which many younger lawyers plan their escape and begin looking for a more positive environment.

2. Case studies: Oliver and Lionel

'Oliver' is a baby boomer and the managing partner of a large firm. At a meeting in his 65th-floor office, he said:

> *There is much talk from younger lawyers about how demanding law firms are. They say we are unrelenting with our associates. Yes, we expect them to work hard. We are not asking them to do anything that we didn't have to do when we began. I believe that many of the younger lawyers are villainising their firms, and I've had enough of it.*

> *These statements are just not factual. Law firms are businesses, not country clubs! With that said, we need to find an answer. What is happening now with differing points of view and turnover is not sustainable.*
>
> *It's my job, along with the executive committee, to keep the lights on, show a profit and take care of my clients. Now there is constant talk that we work our associates too hard. They say we are behind on technology and that our ideas are old-fashioned. To be honest, I'm sick of all of this adversity and hidden agendas.*

This is the dilemma that Oliver and other law firm partners face.

2.1 For every 20 associates hired, 15 leave

According to a study conducted by the NALP Foundation for Law Career Research and Education and the recruiting firm Major Lindsey & Africa, the average attrition rate among associates was 18% between 2012 and 2018.[17]

It is easy to see why Oliver was concerned. According to the same study, over 54% of the associates who left were still considered desirable employees by the firm. Firms would have preferred that they stay. Indeed, firms only wanted 24% of lawyers to leave. The turnover for lawyers of colour and women was even higher, which we will discuss in another chapter.

2.2 Why do young lawyers leave?

Table 7. Reasons for leaving

	Entry Level	Lateral
Work quality standards	13%	18%
Change in legal career	16%	16%
Unmet productivity standards	9%	12%
Hired by a client	10%	11%
Geographic move	14%	9%
Pursuit of a practice area	17%	12%
Better work–life balance	9%	U/K

Source: NALP Foundation and MLA, "Keeping the Keepers IV" (see note 2).

Some 837 law firms provided the data for the study. Between them, participating firms hired more than 27,000 associates and saw more than 20,000 associate departures during the period under study.

According to legal recruiters BCG, it can cost law firms an estimated $200,000 to $500,000 to lose one associate.[18] Attrition can cost a law firm millions. In other words, while the firm is rainmaking and working to bring in more clients and business, millions of dollars are marching out of the back door in associate turnover. It is safe to say that firms are haemorrhaging money.

Oliver realised that a large percentage of the firm's associates would leave:

> *That is why we have to keep associates coming in the door as the others leave. Our talent is vital to our success. Our firm's need for a large labour pool cannot be overstated. If we don't meet our clients' demands, we are out of business. Our firm's talent is synonymous with the quality, capabilities, and output of our organisation.*
>
> *Without associates to do the required work, including massive research, document discovery and the like, we could not accomplish our primary goals. If the firm closes down or goes out of business, maybe everyone can have balance and workable hours, but we will all be out of work. I can't understand why the younger lawyers can't see this. At times it is infuriating.*

2.3 The costs of hiring

The costs of lawyer recruitment and attrition take an increasing toll on every firm's bottom line. The largest law firms spend billions of dollars each year to recruit, train and then lose lawyers from their ranks. Let's take a hypothetical example.

A law firm hires 'Lionel' as an associate, with a salary of $160,000; but this is the culmination of a lengthy process.

The recruiting department must first vet the associate. They must make sure that the candidate will be acceptable before even starting the vetting process. Ranking is an essential component – the ranking of the school, where the candidate ranked in his or her class – as is consideration of the question, Does he or she fit the firm culture?

The interview process begins with several potential candidates. Depending on which practice group Lionel and others will potentially work within, partners will be assigned to the interview process. There will be several interviews with partners, department heads and supervisors before a final decision is made. If the firm used a recruiter they will have negotiated a fee, generally 25% of the salary.

Once the firm decides to hire Lionel, he will begin the onboarding process with the professional development department, and someone will be assigned to help him acclimatise. Partners and associates will normally take time out of their schedules to help the associate adapt to the firm's procedures and culture.

The costs could potentially look like those in Table 8:

Table 8: Associate hiring costs ($)[19]

Associate salary	$160,000
Partner recruiting time (100 hours @ billable rate of $500/hr)	$50,000
Training (270 partner hrs @ $500.00/hr)	$135,000
100 associate hrs @ $200.00/hr	$20,000
Recruiting fee (25% of salary)	$40,000
Total loss due to associate attrition	**$405,000**

Source: Figures derived from various sources (see note 19).

Note that the figures do not include the front-end onboarding costs of administration, human resources and training and development, which could easily total $5–10,000 for a new hire.

Now that Lionel is hired, there will be 'lost' time in getting him up to speed, checking his work and explaining why some things are done a particular way. Someone has to help this young man become a full-fledged lawyer who could, one day, become a valuable asset to the firm.

If Lionel leaves the firm within the first three to five years, the cost of onboarding and training him will have been anything from $425,000 to more than $800,000 (if he is an experienced lawyer).

It is reported that turnover costs the top 400 US law firms around $9.1 billion annually.[20]

2.4 The solution

Our advice to Oliver was to consider the analogy of a cruise liner.

A large cruise liner has over 1,000 crew. Each crew member has a job that is important to providing an excellent and safe voyage for the passengers. The liner is American, with an all English-speaking crew and passengers; but as the cruise continues the English-speaking crew members leave and are replaced by Italian speakers with little knowledge of English. Over time, the Italian speakers make up 60% of the crew. Human resources knew when they took them on that these employees spoke Italian and had different customs. They also knew that neither captain nor senior crew spoke or understood Italian.

A dilemma then arises. The Italian-speaking employees want to observe the siesta – a custom that the ship does not typically follow. There is potential friction between the ship's captain, senior crew, and the new workers. Yet the ship must continue to its destination and provide the passengers with the highest level of service.

The captain's problem is similar to Oliver's. The captain has to somehow find a way to get the ship's employees on the same page if he is to service the needs of the passengers. Likewise, Oliver, the managing partner, needs to remove the cultural and emotional barriers among his lawyers.

"Law firms need to view the problem of inter-generational communication through a new lens."

The upshot for the captain is that the Italian-speaking employees move on. But they are replaced by more Italian speakers because these represent the only available labour pool.

Whether Oliver likes it or not the new, younger lawyers are from a different generation, a different world. Their customs and world view – even their 'language' – are fundamentally different to Oliver's, and they will find it challenging to adapt to some of the firm's policies and traditions. Gen X and millennials come from a technological generation, post-2008 recession and soon post-pandemic world. The two are as different as the Italian- and English-speaking crew on the liner.

When the captain made the mistake of telling the Italian-speaking crew that it was his way or the highway, he was making a fundamental mistake, inviting high turnover, disruption of service and a constant cycle of losing existing crew members and training new ones.

3. Summary

It can be valuable to seek solutions beyond the confines of the law firm model, and the cruise ship analogy struck a chord with Oliver. He now saw the generational problem as akin to a language and cultural barrier. He then resolved not to apportion blame or to take things personally. Like the captain of the liner, he only had one labour pool on which to draw, and no amount of frustration or finger-pointing would change its basic character. He must look elsewhere for solutions.

In short, law firms need to view the problem of inter-generational communication through a new lens.

VI. Being lawyerly can be a problem

1. What being lawyerly means

When we think of a lawyer, we think of someone who practises law; and we assume that he or she will be a trained professional, qualified to offer advice about the law or to represent us in legal matters.

It's clear from over 25 years of coaching lawyers that many share similar qualities. Lawyers tend to have high IQ – but lower EQ – levels and to be:

- good communicators;
- intelligent and analytical;
- cautious;
- quick to assign fault;
- judgemental;
- critical;
- curious;
- passionate and committed; and
- defensive or offensive depending on the context.

This list of qualities is by no means exhaustive, but taken together they represent what is meant in the present context by 'lawyerly' – those qualities upon which law school training builds in order to prepare lawyers for the challenges of practice. The term offers a useful shorthand when making particular points to clients.

These strengths can be effective in helping lawyers during research and discovery, interpreting and administering the law, representing clients, presenting a case in written or verbal form and filing lawsuits.

On the other hand, these same skills can destroy marriages and estrange children, wider relatives and friends. Lawyers can be unforgiving of the past offences of others. They can readily write off an offender using their offensive, defensive, judgemental and analytical skills – all the while assigning blame.

Let's face it, a lawyer's job is to find out who is at fault, take a side (usually the individual who hires them) and proceed to build a case to prove that it is either the other individual's fault or that it is not the fault of the client.

2. Results of being lawyerly

Case study: Jennifer

Lawyerly qualities can wreak havoc on personal relationships; and things can be more complicated when two lawyers marry. Such unions are common among law firms, and they usually present more challenges than others.

Take 'Jennifer', a new law firm associate who strongly believes in hard work to achieve her professional goals. She performed very well in law school and secured a job in a law firm in which she saw a potential future. But what she wasn't prepared for was rivalry among associates, even of the same generation – in the case of her firm, millennial versus millennial.

Jennifer found herself sidelined in the firm when another millennial associate sought to position himself favourably with a firm partner, at her expense. In Jennifer's case, her associate colleague put his ambition first and constantly sought to curry favour with the partner in charge of their practice group, attending to his needs and deliberately keeping other associates like Jennifer out of important work and projects and in the dark about practice group decision making.

This stoked resentment from Jennifer and hurt her feelings. She considered leaving the firm. None of the associates had been guided, through mentoring or otherwise, as to how to deal with such behaviour. As Jennifer saw it, teamwork had been sidelined in favour of personal ambition, and her hopes and dreams for the firm were now up in the air.

3. IQ versus EQ

IQ (intelligence quotient) and EQ (emotional quotient or emotional intelligence) are two very different measurements. The legal profession focuses primarily on IQ.

Developing one's IQ is imperative for a good lawyer. Since it is a competitive profession, being sharp mentally, analytically and verbally are key ingredients for success.

Lawyers compete in their firms, within their profession and with opposing counsel; there is always a ranking, even if it's invisible. They tend to compare themselves to each other, often in the context of the prestige of the firm. Lawyers may secretly even assess each other according to the area of law they practise, the types of client they represent, their hourly rates, the car they drive, where they live and their standing within the legal community, locally, nationally and internationally.

Habits of comparison, status and ranking that began in law school persist through most of a lawyer's career. Unfortunately, these markers do not include emotional intelligence, which contributes to contentment, harmonious relationships and a sense of feeling connected.

Outward symbols of success are too important to many lawyers. In extreme cases, a lack of the accoutrements can lead to substance abuse, alcoholism and depression, which can in turn contribute to harsh judgement of others who lawyers perceive to be not up to their standards. These proclivities towards ranking and comparisons bleed over into generational differences, including harsh judgements from boomers, Gen Xers and millennials alike.

4. Why emotional intelligence is important

Studies have shown that while lawyers can score very highly on the IQ rating, they have a below-average EQ score. EQ can be generally defined as the ability to:

- be aware of one's emotions and feelings;
- express one's emotions and interpersonal communications; and
- handle personal relationships judiciously, with empathy and compassion.

Lawyers are trained in analytical thinking but not in emotional intelligence. Over-emphasis on analytical thought chokes out the key ingredients that build close relationships – one reason that lawyers have a high rate of divorce.

In the United States, it has been shown that lawyers are much more likely to become divorced than people in other careers – and even more so in Big Law.[21] There are many reasons, but the primary indicator is that these lawyers spend more time and energy on their law firm relationships than their relationships with their spouses.

Case study: Fred
'Fred' is considered a fine lawyer by his law firm and his legal community. He is very active and enjoys his law practice. Although Fred enjoys his success, he has often been disgruntled by the "stupidity or carelessness" of others.

The problem with being constantly disappointed by others is that such sentiments have a tendency to repeat themselves. Over the years, Fred included many secretaries, paralegals and young associates on his list.

As time passed and the millennials came on the scene, Fred lambasted these so-called "cry babies" and included them on his list. He felt contempt for those he did not respect or who he felt were ineffective.

As with all habits, this way of judging folks bled over into his home life. Although Fred provided an excellent lifestyle for his family, he was not fun to be around at home. His relationships were all strained. In short, Fred was not happy; and his family were unhappy when Fred was home.

When Fred was made aware that he lacked empathy and compassion – emotional intelligence – he determined to change.

5. Characteristics of emotional intelligence
People in general, and lawyers in particular, who possess a high degree of emotional intelligence tend to share the following characteristics:

Open-mindedness: Open-minded lawyers want to learn how to accept new experiences, ideas and people easily. The law has long held on to traditions, so this can be challenging.

Ability to articulate feelings/emotions: When a lawyer has an analytical mindset, they can easily disassociate their feelings. Indeed, it is considered an asset in the law to divorce oneself from one's emotions.

A lawyer with a high EQ will not only know their emotions – they will also be able to describe them to others. This requires leaving analysis and judgement behind and is a communication strength at work and at home.

"A lawyer with a high EQ will seek to understand and communicate their own feelings, but also to understand the feelings of others."

Capacity for empathy: A lawyer with a high EQ will seek to understand and communicate their own feelings, but also to understand the feelings of others. Developing this as a strength reduces friction and misunderstanding. It creates harmony at the office and at home.

Lawyers with a narcissistic tendency will have little ability to empathise with others. They will tend to be more selfish and self-involved, usually unable to understand what other people are feeling. They will rarely be apologetic, remorseful or guilty.

Observational skill: An observant lawyer will be involved or interested in others' needs. They will show concern and be able to discern social cues to attend to the needs of others, at work or at home.

Ability to lead by example: Unlike Fred, in our story earlier in this chapter, a lawyer with a high EQ will lead by example. This lawyer will display compassion instead of categorising employees, judging or shunning them. Instead, they will lead by example. No one learns by constant lectures, criticisms, or shunning.

Active listening skills: Active listening, with the commitment to comprehend what others are actually saying, is an indicator of a high EQ. When a lawyer seeks to understand others, they set aside the key tools lawyers learn: analysis, judgement and looking for blame or a verdict.

Lawyers are generally good listeners because they make a living listening to the evidence. However, there is a difference between listening and hearing. Many lawyers listen through their analytical or judgement ears – they hear their interlocutor but don't necessarily understand what they really mean.

Personal motivation/willingness to grow: Lawyers who seek to improve their EQ will enjoy the process of personal growth and learning more about themselves. These lawyers understand how this gives them an edge when overcoming obstacles at home and within the firm.

Some lawyers, especially boomers, might decide that they are too old to change. We know that science has demonstrated our brains' plasticity. The science of neuroplasticity shows that learning new things keeps individuals young, enthusiastic and enjoying life to the full.

Experience shows that the lawyers who embrace change and are willing to laugh at former behaviours that were not in their best interests, or those of their firms and families, have rich and satisfying practices beyond anything they could have hoped for.

Helpfulness: People with high EQs help others, investing time and energy without an agenda, and the rewards they receive are immense.

Too many lawyers have hidden agendas. When approached by younger or less experienced lawyers, they may feel someone is imposing upon their valuable time. They are less than accommodating towards family members, including their children. They start from the position that everyone should "figure it out themselves".

Balance: Although some lawyers are aggravated by talk of work–life balance, there is increasing awareness of its importance within the firm. High-EQ people are self-aware – they can readily identify what they need to attain that balance.

Having said that, there are still lawyers who feel that considering work–life balance is babysitting – pandering to young lawyers who are lazy and don't want to make the necessary sacrifices.

Transparency: High-EQ individuals value honesty, whether it is high stakes ethics or being completely honest with the progression of a project. With a conducive environment at work and home, people are less likely to hide the truth from you. By setting an example, the lawyer creates an environment where they can count on a high-EQ person to tell the truth.

Lawyers who insist on a judgemental, analytical, 'just the facts' approach will find themselves living in a bubble, where everyone tells them what they want to hear.

6. Lawyerly behaviours

Lawyers who start from an analytical, judgemental base will miss out on meaningful relationships. They will stunt the growth of others around them and create an atmosphere of right vs wrong, good vs bad, like vs dislike and should vs should not.

Case study: Jerome

'Jerome' studied psychology before attending law school. This experience, he says, allows him to be attuned to what he sees around him at work. He has observed how much lawyers can negatively impact firm morale by not being sensitive to the needs of other professionals in the firm, including secretarial, marketing and other support staff.

Such staff members often occupy senior positions and are very knowledgeable about, for example, internal practices; they can be strong allies to junior lawyers. But Jerome has witnessed junior lawyers treating staff disrespectfully, squandering opportunities for team building and trust.

A little sensitivity – that's to say, emotional intelligence – by junior lawyers will go a long way, he suggests, towards building alliances, goodwill and morale among everyone at a firm, not just lawyers.

7. Summary

We can see from this chapter that 'lawyerly' tends to mean high IQ and linear thinking; but these attributes on their own will result in adversarial, contentious relationships with little room for growth. Lawyers need to put more emphasis on developing their emotional intelligence.

The lawyer who is committed to bridging the gap between the generations, as opposed to seeking others to blame, will look to emotional intelligence.

This will be discussed in the next chapter.

VII. Building emotional intelligence – a step towards unity

1. Change is slow

Many lawyers will scoff at the idea of incorporating emotional intelligence into their firms. They don't understand that EQ is an essential ingredient for increased profits and growth.

This attitude tends to militate against fast progress.

Case study: Walter

'Walter' is a managing partner at a mid-sized law firm. In one of our first assessment conversations, he had this to say:

> *We are here to make money. Our law firm is a business that has done very well up until now. We don't have time to talk about IQ or EQ!*
>
> *We have to serve our clients, and that is the bottom line. Let the professional development folks put on a couple of webinars or seminars and we will be fine.*

That attitude was precisely the problem. To create harmony and unity between the generations took more than lip service, otherwise things would get worse, not better.

Walter was asked to imagine a military unit about to fight a battle. Did a battalion with a unified mindset have a better chance of victory than one where the soldiers were at odds? Of course, the unit whose soldiers had each other's backs would tend to triumph. The same principle applies within a law firm. Solving the inner friction was a necessary component to increasing productivity and profits.

Walter may have been irritated by the analogy, but he leaned in to learn more.

A few changes in attitude can make an enormous difference.

2. Passing EQ to professional development won't work

Take this scenario: professional development or human resources offer a class, webinar or seminar. A few folk break away from their busy day to attend. Or, if the class is mandatory, lawyers show up reluctantly. Many times, management are too busy. The attendees learn a few headline points which are all but forgotten in less than a week.

The firm has ticked the proverbial box. Now they have addressed emotional intelligence versus intelligence quotient. Everyone is pleased.

But the truth is that nothing has changed. The paradigm or the culture of the firm has to change from the inside out and the top down. Change begins with:

- the managing partner;
- the management committee;
- chairpersons of the various practice groups; and
- section heads and supervisors.

Studies reveal that organisations with EQ perform better – a genuine commitment followed by action steps will increase productivity and profits. According to the American Psychological Association, emotional intelligence offers a bridge between the generations within the firm.[22]

Before a team can work well, the management in the firm has to create a structure, or culture, which will dictate how the firm is run.

Emotional intelligence should be part of this structure, which will generally mean expanding the firm's foundational values to include a culture of cooperation and encouragement. The new culture will be underpinned by:

- mutual understanding;
- valuing individuals, no matter who they are;
- allowing individuals to have their own opinions; and
- respectfully agreeing to disagree.

3. The beginning of EQ in your firm

Let's take the example of a football team. The team begins to build team spirit by building trust. If team members feel belittled, minimised and criticised, there is no trust. They will be nervous, afraid to make mistakes. They will avoid taking risks. And these factors will inhibit and stunt the team as a whole.

For a team to work well, the team members must:

- feel comfortable with each other;
- have sufficient trust to cooperate with each other;
- foster an environment where members try to understand each other;
- work within a culture where they are appreciated; and
- know that appreciation comes from the top down.

When these elements are in place, each individual feels secure. They take risks; they strive to be valued team members. This transformation cannot be a haphazard, one-and-done exercise.

"Before a team can work well, the management in the firm has to create a structure, or culture, which will dictate how the firm is run."

Any team – indeed any firm – that seriously incorporates these values into its culture will soar.

Studies have shown that job performance correlates with emotional intelligence, and that individuals with higher EQ scores perform better than those with high IQ alone.[23]

Group intelligence makes a big difference with small things. A firm significantly reduces its turnover with a culture of:

- appreciation;
- respect;
- honour; and
- encouragement.

Contrast this with the current atmosphere in most law firms. When emotional intelligence is prioritised, the atmosphere breeds enthusiasm lost due to prolonged stress and anxiety. Lawyers recall their original love of the law. They look forward to getting to the office. They feel as if they are on a unified mission. Stress, tension and anxiety are significantly reduced.

These principles apply equally to solo practices, mid-sized firms and Big Law, and their application will be transformational for non-traditional law firms and law schools.

VIII. Friction in the context of diversity, equity and inclusion

1. Gender

Case study: Rebecca

It is our experience that, in general, the gender gap is real and that women lawyers find equal opportunity with regard to business development to be elusive.

Many firms hire a diversity and inclusion professional. But is this enough?

'Rebecca' is a junior lawyer in a large law firm. A top graduate of a major law school, she had ambitions to become a rainmaking partner. But the firm she works for, like many other large law firms, is characterised by frequent power plays and rivalries around business development – specifically, in relation to so-called 'origination credit', where one or several lawyers are identified as being the ones responsible for identifying and helping to bring in a new client.

In Rebecca's firm, these rivalries lead to power struggles and acrimony between partners. Rebecca and her other ambitious associate colleagues like to participate in business development activities. They are drawn in on many occasions and asked to take sides. When partners fight over origination and seek support for their side of the argument, Rebecca and her associate colleagues feel powerless. These power plays stoke resentment and hurt morale. Sometimes other senior lawyers intervene to save junior lawyers, but not always.

Rebecca is now considering a lateral move to another firm which takes a more cooperative, collegiate approach to business development.

2. Bridging the gap with diversity and inclusion

There are approximately 146,000 practising solicitors in the United Kingdom,[24] and more than 1.3 million lawyers in the United States.[25]

White, non-Hispanic lawyers account for 85% of US lawyers.[26] As of 2021, 37% of the lawyers in the United States were women.[27]

Case study: Dennis, Natalie and Catherine

These young lawyers' stories illustrate how many law firms throughout the United States are structured.

'Dennis' explained how, after his early experiences, being a hiring manager became his calling. He graduated from an Ivy League law school along with two friends. 'Natalie' is Caucasian like Dennis, and 'Catherine' is African American. Catherine ranked among the top of their class.

> *They both were better students than I was. We became good friends from the moment we met in orientation. We studied together, and quite frankly, they saved me many times when I might have failed. The three of us would all go for an all-night study together with pizza and beer. On our days off, we watched the games on Sundays. We were all in over our heads and it was nice to be with friends who understood.*
>
> *I was hired right out of school as well as my two friends Natalie and Catherine. As luck would have it, Catherine and I were both employed at the same firm.*
>
> *We all graduated and eventually got married around the same time and began to have children. Our spouses fit into our group and we were like one happy family. But things started to change. These changes caused a strain in my friendships with Natalie and Catherine.*
>
> *I could tell that something was going on. The firm gave me a great mentor and much support. I often left earlier than Catherine, even*

though my ambitious friend brought in a very substantial client. It didn't seem to matter. I could tell she was struggling.

As the years went along, I received privileges that I didn't deserve. Catherine worked much harder than I did, and truthfully, she was a better lawyer. Meanwhile, I kept receiving promotions, working on great projects and cases. It is evident that they were grooming me to become a junior partner, and later a partner.

Whenever I saw my friend Catherine, she felt isolated. Day after day, she was doing research and discovery. I think the last straw was when our families were together during the Christmas holidays one year. I slipped and mentioned to Catherine about my big bonus. She found out how much more money I made than her.

Catherine confided to Dennis that she was going to leave the firm:

I love our firm, but you and I both know I work more hours because fewer of my hours are considered billable. I make less money than you. You've said I am a better lawyer than you!

I have not advanced; I have been ignored. I am not blind. I can see all the opportunities you have received. I am leaving and starting my own firm. Maybe not today, but we are working towards that; my husband and I are saving money. I want to leave, and the sooner, the better.

Within 18 months, Catherine had left the firm. And for a while their relationship was strained.

Of his friend Natalie, Dennis said:

I lost track of Natalie, my other classmate. One day, I heard that Natalie was leaving the practice of law altogether and becoming a lawyer recruiter. We had both been with our firms for well over fifteen years. I thought this was a big mistake. I met her for lunch to try to convince her not to throw away her career as a lawyer.

And for her part, Natalie – by all accounts one of the brightest senior associates in her firm – said to us that she had felt isolated and unsupported in her firm. She had been in a silo doing research and discovery, and told us:

I remember in law school, we all had these dreams of being great lawyers with a big law firm. But that was a pipe dream, and there is no way my firm will give me a fair chance to be the great lawyer I was meant to be.

Dennis was disheartened that such outdated office politics and policies should risk depriving the profession of bright and committed lawyers. Catherine and Natalie, he said, were better lawyers than he was. He resolved that any time he was in a position to do so, he would champion diversity, inclusion and equity for women and minorities in his firm.

2.1 Legacy structures

To fully understand why this equity blind spot in larger firms is more common than we might imagine, we need to go back in time and examine certain foundational structures, and why they endure even today.

IX. The history of diversity in elite firms

1. Formation of white-shoe firms

The foundation stone of law firms everywhere, and certainly in the United States, was traditionally status. These elite and exclusive organisations are known as 'white-shoe' firms, and have historically looked after legal matters for Fortune 500 corporations.

Lawyers who graduated from Ivy League schools represented academic excellence. Legal institutions, conforming to rigorous admissions policies, included only the social elite and historically followed discriminatory practices in the areas of gender and race.

Many of the direct offshoots of these white-shoe firms, like their progenitors, consisted of White Anglo-Saxon Protestants (WASPs), a term with anti-Semitic connotations – white-shoe firms were off-limits for Jews until 1960. Their cultures reflected the exclusionary tendencies of the original white-shoe firms. There were only limited opportunities for Jewish and Catholic lawyers, as well as other non-WASPs. Women and people of colour weren't even a remote consideration.

Times have changed in terms of discrimination, but the term 'white-shoe' persists, still somewhat defined as a law firm owned and run by members of the WASP elite. These WASP lawyers are generally conservative. A 2010 article in *The Economist* described 'white-shoe' as being synonymous with "big, old, traditional and east-coast".[28]

For decades, elite meant WASPs (and later Jewish males of 'high pedigree') only. This exclusivity translated to no women, no people of colour and no minorities. And arguably the bottom line is that these firms are to this day considered to be the gold standard, the model that all firms aspire to.

2. Questions law firms should ask

When a firm has a diverse group of lawyers, they provide better services for clients. Different experiences, understanding and perspectives bring benefits to every client relationship.

Today, most prominent law firms have a named diversity, equity and inclusion (DEI) manager. We applaud this as a good start, but it's worth asking a few specific questions to gain a deeper perspective:

- What direct actions has the management taken to build equity and inclusion?
- Has the management committee designed and executed a strategic plan, or does the firm practice diversity and inclusion in name only?

"When a firm has a diverse group of lawyers, they provide better services for clients. Different experiences, understanding and perspectives bring benefits to every client relationship."

- How does the management committee empower and support the DEI manager?
- Has the management committee considered the scale of the DEI person's task in educating a group of 86% white-majority lawyers?[29]
- Is it possible that without a management committee designed and deployed framework, shared analysis and language, along with a strategic plan, efforts towards DEI will fail?
- Does the firm's management committee measure success in DEI based on how many women and non-majority lawyers are hired, while ignoring attrition and turnover rates?
- Has hiring non-majority lawyers solved the problem or reinforced the belief that they don't fit the firm's culture?
- What is the management committee of the firm doing to build more leaders to include women and non-majority lawyers?

Change is hard, especially in the legal profession.

3. Women lawyers and bias

Although much has improved, women's representation in the legal profession is still a work in progress. Regardless of nationality, race or background, women have shared similar experiences of gender bias and discrimination.

A number of women have been barrier-breakers. Following a court challenge, Arabella Mansfield became the first woman to be admitted to the Iowa Bar, in 1869, the state amending its licensing statute to admit women and minorities. Helena Normanton scored a remarkable number of firsts in her legal career, gaining a first-class degree from the University of London and being called to the English bar in 1922 to become the first woman to practise as a barrister.

Fast forward to 2019. Approximately 64% of lawyers are men, 36% women. Women face multiple biases, some 'double-barrelled' (as, for example, when a woman behaves in a 'feminine' way and she is liked, but not respected or seen as a leader; or when she behaves in a 'masculine' way and she is judged, or even disliked). Either way, she loses.

According to the National Association for Law Placement, Inc (NALP), 16% of lawyers in US law firms identify as either racial and ethnic minorities, and 35% as women.[30] These numbers speak for themselves.

There are a number of recommendations that law firms could implement to keep women lawyers:

- Assess the impact of firm policies and practices on women lawyers.

- Take steps to ensure there is a critical mass of women partners on key firm committees.
- Increase lateral hiring of women partners.
- Provide resources to relieve pressures from family obligations.
- Be cognisant that there are pressures that women face more often than their male colleagues.
- Be flexible enough to support changing practices.

4. Representation by race, ethnicity and gender

People of colour, women in particular, continue to make slow progress in terms of representation at major US law firms:

- The percentage of black partners is 2%.
- The percentage of black associates is 5%.
- Black and Latinx women make up less than 1% of all partners.
- Black women associates make up 3.04% of law firm lawyers.[31]

5. Double-barrelled biases

Tired tropes and stereotypes persist:

- Black/African American women are regularly pegged as angry or shrill when they become expressive.
- Latinas are similarly stereotyped as quick-tempered and excitable.
- Asian women are in some cases viewed as passive or invisible.

6. Solutions

Here are some solutions to these ongoing problems:

- Commit to diversity, equity and inclusion. This commitment requires more than ticking the box of hiring diverse lawyers and then when they leave, saying, "We tried".
- Build a culture of diversity, equity and inclusion. Focus on what it takes to retain lawyers from diverse backgrounds and genders.
- Given that equity means shared power, include diverse lawyers in leadership and management and learn from their perspectives.
- Emphasise retention more than simply hiring diverse lawyers.
- Management committees should institute DEI procedures that are more than box-ticking exercises.
- Management committee members should roll up their sleeves and do the work to transform their current DEI situation.

DEI strategies need to include:

- growth opportunities;
- equal compensation;

- leadership pathways; and
- mentoring for women, blacks and other people of colour.

7. The Mansfield Rule[32]

The Mansfield Rule (named after Arabella Mansfield – see above), which inspired the 2016 Women in Law Hackathon,[33] measures whether a law firm is committed to DEI according to the following criteria:

- Does the firm have at least 30% women lawyers who are either:
  - lawyers of colour;
  - LGBTQ; and/or
  - lawyers with disabilities?
- Are they:
  - in leadership and governance roles;
  - in equity partnership;
  - being promoted;
  - included in formal pitch opportunities; and/or
  - in senior lateral positions?

The goal of the Mansfield Rule is to boost representation of diverse lawyers in law firm leadership, emphasising that diversity, equity and inclusion includes more than hiring a DEI manager, additional women and people of colour, and LGBTQ or disabled lawyers.

The management committee must want to lead, and hiring consultants and coaches, as well as leading the way towards the Mansfield Rule's incorporation, will make an enormous difference.

It is important that millennials, as a more diverse generation, are included in these new approaches to DEI.

8. Summary

There is still much work to be done in the legal profession in the areas of gender, diversity, inclusion and equity for all lawyers, not least to address generational differences in the context of DEI with a view to encouraging unity and harmony within law firms.

But it is not all bad news. The encouragement and promotion of young women in the law is well exemplified by the efforts of Ms. JD, a non-profit organisation "dedicated to the success of aspiring and early career women lawyers".[34] This organisation's aims are summarised on its website as follows:

> *Ms. JD celebrates women's achievements, addresses remaining challenges and facilitates continued progress by bringing legal practitioners and law students together to share in an ongoing conversation about gender issues in law school and the profession.*[35]

X. The consequences of persisting generational friction

1. Introduction

This chapter will look at the consequences of friction, and therefore turnover, within the different generations – one of the biggest expenses faced by today's law firms. In particular, we will examine:

- firms' acknowledgement that change needs to occur;
- the important first step to building a better corporate culture; and
- the consequences of the current law firm turnover dilemma.

We believe that a firm takes a big step in the right direction when management admits that generational differences affect morale, productivity and profits. Once we come out of denial, we can look at what are the liabilities and costs of continuing to let the gap between generations exist.

Before making the necessary changes, owners and managers need to identify the areas where the problem manifests itself, as explored below.

2. Hiring and training costs

An online assessment of more than 1,400 respondents was conducted by The Right Profile and JD Match,[36] which provides some interesting figures to consider when seeking an estimate of what it costs when a firm hires a new associate.

Table 9: Cost of hiring an associate

Cost to recruit one first year associate	$250,000
Cost to the firm when an associate leaves	$400,000
Approximate rate of annual attrition	17%
Associates who leave in first 3 years	46%
Lawyers who leave within first 5 years	81%
Laterals who lose money for the firm	43%
Annual loss for a 400-lawyer firm	$25 million +

Source: Figures derived from various sources and quoted in Levin and MacEwen, "Assessing Lawyer Traits" (see note 36).

The report demonstrates that the strategies many law firms employ are flawed and outdated, especially in the age of Gen X and millennials. Hiring practices, onboarding and training programmes must be re-examined with a view to the potential costs.

When a new lawyer is hired, a firm invests significant time, money and resources in the hiring and training process – 95% of hiring partners say that newly hired associates just out of law school lack the basic skills needed to perform their jobs.[37] Comprehensive training is required by partners and other lawyers. Time spent answering questions and familiarising the new hire in law firm protocol, the law and essential procedures, adds up.

This represents a large front-end investment for the firm, with little immediate financial return – given the costs of hiring and training, it can take up to five years for a new hire to become profitable. In the first two years of practice alone, as previously stated, with ongoing training and reduced productivity new associates can cost between $200,000 and $500,000.[38]

Included in this figure are:

- recruitment fees;
- partner's time spent interviewing;

- partner training;
- associate-to-associate training;
- reduced productivity of associates training the new hire;
- limited productivity by the new hire as they learn their job; and
- miscellaneous costs.

In terms of attrition and turnover, millennials are a particular problem. These young lawyers change jobs at a disconcerting pace. Boomer and Gen X lawyers, for the most part, patiently paid their dues, but millennial lawyers tend to vote with their feet. They quit to demonstrate their discontent or unhappiness – indeed, not just when they are unhappy but when they are not happy enough – and do not hesitate to try a new firm, or even a new career.

One law firm owner who was tired of the revolving door said to us, "Why didn't they tell me they were unhappy? I am sick and tired of these folks not saying anything about their discontent and I don't find out until they give me their notice. It makes me so angry!"

He is not alone.

Increased turnover, then – depending on the generation – results in:

- slower growth;
- loss of competitive edge; and
- reduced profits.

3. Changing workforce dynamics

It is unwise to ignore the changing dynamics within the legal workforce. At one time, retaining law firm talent involved offering competitive compensation and a steady workload. However, much has changed in recent years.

Notably, while law school graduates are entering practice in record numbers, the proportion of high-level graduates has decreased. Therefore, there is record demand for the top 20% of law school graduates, and these young lawyers are recruited aggressively. In this competitive environment, if law firms do not offer these lawyers a strong sense of fulfilment it is unlikely the top talent will stay.

Turnover will be a constant problem unless firms adapt.

4. Low workforce morale

When law firms experience faster turnover, workloads increase among the remaining lawyers, and this leads to longer hours, low morale, stress, anxiety and depression. Emergencies arise from efforts to determine where the departed lawyer left off.

"We are all products of our generations and backgrounds. While the legal profession has a shared language learned in law school, there are ways of communicating common to some generations that may grate on others."

Furthermore, when clients become aware that lawyers are frequently leaving a firm it can damage a firm's reputation. Clients are used to communicating with one person in the firm and if they suddenly leave, trust can be undermined. If it occurs several times, the client relationship can be at risk.

Senior lawyers and partners are affected too. Often, the initial training falls to the partners, who have a high hourly billing rate. They must sacrifice time to train a new associate on the one hand, while striving to maintain profitability on the other.

It can be extremely discouraging when a partner sees that their investment has left the firm, as they'll need to start again – searching for, hiring and training new associates. Hundreds of billable hours will have been lost. When this happens several times a year, partners can become frustrated.

Being open to making the necessary changes to accomplish a better work environment can often become key to keeping new associates long after they've been trained.

5. Communication gaps

Turnover can point to a gap between generations in a law firm. When there are no shared values, communication gaps can widen.

For the firm to thrive, lawyers must work together, with effective communication. The ability to speak a common firm language is key to business growth. Virtual staffing, cloud and other advances have conspired to reduce human interaction, and in some cases challenged the nature of communication within firms.

With less physical interaction between lawyers and staff, communication improvement becomes critical for building relationships, both in the office environment and with clients. Likewise, good communication between the generations helps to enhance human engagement and ensure client satisfaction.

Effective communication is the key to growth for any business, including the legal industry.

6. Different conversation styles

We are all products of our generations and backgrounds. While the legal profession has a shared language learned in law school, there are ways of communicating common to some generations that may grate on others.

For example, boomers may over-explain to Gen Xers and see millennials as a texting culture, lacking diplomacy.

Key to overcoming these differences of views about communication is to learn to not misinterpret, and to be compassionate and understanding.

7. Communication in the context of COVID-19

Never before have all firms, all around the world, been at or near a standstill save for remote working, with spouses and young children at home while lawyers struggled to save their practices.

Courts were closed, so litigation lawyers suddenly found that they were unable to practise, and the reduction in human engagement, along with the rise of cloud technology and virtual working, made it more difficult to effectively communicate with colleagues.

Zoom meetings alone have been insufficient to replace in-person communication, and misunderstandings caused by greater emphasis on email communications have placed strain on some practices. Different ideas between the generations about how to use Zoom have produced confusion – some senior lawyers prefer no cameras, while young lawyers thrive in an environment where video is the default. The end result is frustration between lawyers of different generations.

Lawyers who could not handle the isolation suffered, while individuals who preferred their own company thrived.

Micromanagement in the office in the new era of remote working has created an environment where lawyers and staff dread using the office at all – and turnover is worse.

Many of the top law firms have been eager to bring lawyers back into the office, and many millennials have balked. They have proven that they can be productive by working remotely, but for law firms this hasn't always been good enough.

A concerted effort will help everyone adjust to the new, post-pandemic normal and will go a long way to repairing communication gaps in every firm.

8. Summary

Immediate steps to change the model of the law firm's hiring, training and retaining model must be addressed. The most important first step is to acknowledge the ways in which disparate areas of the firm have been affected by inter-generational friction.

XI. Throwing money at the problem will not solve the conflicts

1. Introduction

Law firms have come to realise that throwing money at the problem of generational differences to increase retention does not work.

We can agree that there is dissatisfaction from all generations – millennials, baby boomers and Gen Xers – and that only by breaking down the source of the complaints and discarding those approaches that have been unsuccessful, will we find solutions.

2. The complaints

Some senior lawyers have these complaints about their younger counterparts:

- They are needy.
- They lack motivation.
- They expect instant gratification.
- They want quick promotions and accolades.
- They put too much importance on work–life balance.
- They constantly complain about the technology.
- They complain about needing more flexibility.
- They want more mentorship.
- They ask for 360-degree feedback.
- They say they need more office engagement.

3. Failed/counterproductive approaches

A number of practices – and proposed solutions – are distinctly unhelpful:

- increasing salaries;
- emphasising billable hours;
- working multiple all-nighters;
- stigmatising lawyers who work fewer hours;
- enabling a toxic firm culture;
- allowing wealthy partners to hoard clients;
- providing no incentive/recognition for being a team player;
- blaming others/throwing them under the bus;
- instituting half-hearted mentorship programmes;
- penalising women lawyers after maternity leave;
- treating women as workhorses while men leave for happy hour;
- tolerating gender bias;
- fostering and old-school culture;
- accepting unfairness, poor communication and lack of transparency; or
- devaluing respect, collegiality and kindness.

4. Approaches for lawyer retention and conflict resolution

4.1 Acknowledge change

As baby boomers look forward to eventually retiring, there is a heavy – and two-way – responsibility to resolve inter-generational issues. A chasm exists but it is not unbridgeable.

Understanding the motivations and aspirations of other generations, and accepting change, will weaken posturing and any urge to dominate.

4.2 Engage associates through teamwork

Fostering of teamwork is among the immediate steps law firms can take to connect with, inspire, motivate and retain millennials. Research shows that quick access to other members of their practice group or team helps associates find guidance and support – or simply feel more included.

Effective teamwork produces results:

- It creates synergy and a sense of loyalty to the team and the firm.
- It is more efficient and helps lawyers to expedite work quickly.
- It engages associates – and everyone learns leadership skills.
- It promotes a sense of achievement as team members move through matters with speed and enthusiasm.

"As baby boomers look forward to eventually retiring, there is a heavy – and two-way – responsibility to resolve inter-generational issues. A chasm exists but it is not unbridgeable."

- It uses individual skillsets and takes account of each lawyer's strengths and weaknesses.
- It allows each associate to develop a relationship with a partner or firm leader.

4.3 Encourage reverse mentoring

There are no limits to the topics or disciplines that reverse mentoring can impact, beyond sharing knowledge about technology. Reverse mentoring will increase retention, create a team atmosphere, break communication barriers, improve digital knowledge, increase awareness of cultural viewpoints and diversity, and enhance communication and engagement:

> *Reverse mentoring pairs younger employees with executive team members to mentor them on various topics of strategic and cultural relevance ... Reverse mentoring can increase retention, by helping senior lawyers become more sophisticated about social media, drive culture change and promote diversity.*[39]

5. Summary

Expenditure per se, then, is not the solution – increasing salaries at the major AmLaw 100 firms did not solve the retention problem or resolve the differences between the generations.[40]

The problems are intrinsic to the long-established structure of law firms and the culture it creates. The solutions include building more engagement among the ranks by the creation of teams, and reverse mentoring to improve communication and bridge the technology gap between the generations.

XII. Lawyer well-being – good and bad news

1. Introduction

It has not always been the case, but there is one thing on which lawyers of all generations now agree. Baby boomers, Gen Xers and millennials alike desire optimal mental, emotional and physical health. They recognise that good health enables them to be good lawyers.

Despite this, studies indicate that as a profession, lawyers do not meet what might be regarded as minimum standards of good health.[41]

2. Mental, emotional and physical health

Many lawyers in the past did not acknowledge that an essential aspect of overall health includes mental, and therefore emotional, health. The World Health Organization defines mental health as follows:

> *A state of well-being in which the individual realises his or her own abilities, can cope with the normal stresses of life, can work productively and fruitfully, and is able to make a contribution to his or her community.*[42]

And overall health is defined in WHO's Constitution as follows:

> *A state of complete physical, mental and social well-being and not merely the absence of disease or infirmity.*[43]

Conversations about health and well-being provide an opportunity to bridge the communication gap between the generations.

3. Common ground

Given the consensus on the importance of health, all generations can come to the table and make a unified commitment to improve well-being within the firm; indeed, to make well-being central to the firm's approach to productivity and profits.

The legal profession has traditionally ignored health in favour of billable hours and work production. This mindset is changing, and not before time. It has been suggested that almost half of an individual's well-being is dictated by their genes and their environment (upbringing, home environment, career, financial circumstances); but 40% is influenced by choices, attitudes, relationships, received values and sense of purpose[44] – all areas that are open to influence within the structure and culture of the law firm.

4. Law school

Many lawyers mention that law school changed their personality. The young student learns to sacrifice their mental and emotional health to meet the demands of the course. Many turn to alcohol or drugs to cope. One lawyer said, "Law school changes the way you think about everything."

With mental and physical health on the back burner, many experience isolation, a sense of helplessness about how they are judged, a lack of balance between work and other facets of their life, and the pressure of a hyper-competitive environment; all of which can drastically reduce one's self-esteem.

On the plus side, lawyers can readily understand each other since they all went through the rigours of study in a demanding subject, passing the bar and all of the other pressures and competition required to succeed.

5. Well-being and lawyers

Research in the United States has shown that lawyers have higher rates of anxiety, depression and stress compared to other professions. Why is this? It's not that lawyers are genetically predisposed to poorer well-being than others; but there is something about the culture and practice of law that impacts them.

The legal profession's culture is known for poor work–life balance – long hours and coming to work despite illness, injury or mental anxiety. Fear of failure, a competitive environment which began in law school, and a high incidence of perfectionism drives the profession.

"The legal profession has traditionally ignored health in favour of billable hours and work production. This mindset is changing, and not before time."

Lawyers are expected to cope with the demands of the job, and fear that not coping will be seen as a sign of weakness. They can find it difficult to acknowledge that they need support, or to talk openly about mental health in the workplace.

Brian Cuban, author of the best-selling *The Addicted Lawyer: Tales of the Bar, Booze, Blow, and Redemption*,[45] told us:

> *One of the biggest mental health challenges lawyers face as a profession is the reluctance to allow themselves to be vulnerable in safe spaces and to share their struggles.*
>
> *The legal profession tends to view vulnerability as a weakness. The truth is that it is one of the linchpins to recovery. It is also just as important for us to protect each other and step outside of our comfort zone by utilizing the "Two Ask" rule.*
>
> *Ask Number 1; if you see someone you think is struggling, ask: How are you doing?*
>
> *Ask Number 2; You want to offer support so follow up with: Do you know you can come to me if you ever want to talk?*

Here is the rub. You have to mean it and be willing to engage if the person seeks you out because of mental health struggles.

It doesn't mean you are a therapist, but you can educate yourself about the resources available such as the Lawyer Assistance Programs and help provide a path to recovery.

6. ABA report on well-being

When the ABA published the National Task Force on Lawyer Well-Being's "The Path to Lawyer Well-Being: Practical Recommendations for Positive Change",[46] many law firms pledged to focus more on well-being.

As Table 10 shows, the report revealed some startling statistics.

Table 10: Prevalence of factors affecting well-being

Depression	28%
Anxiety	19%
Stress	23%
Alcohol abuse	21%
Suicidal thoughts	11.5%

Source: PR Krill et al, "The Prevalence of Substance Abuse" (see note 46).

These statistics were even higher for law school students.[47]

7. Removing the stigma

Bridging the gap between the generations requires eliminating the stigma that is often associated with mental or emotional health issues.

When individuals in the firm acknowledge that well-being is a priority, everyone will be conscious of their mental and physical health, resulting in a healthier environment where one in every four lawyers, or even more, can feel free to seek the help they need without fear of being labelled, ostracised or seen as a failure.

It takes courage to seek help in a competitive environment where it would normally have been considered a weakness.

8. Well-being and inter-generational communication

All generations face well-being issues, which puts everyone on the same page in seeking help. Meetings and committees in which all generations are represented can discuss and implement changes.

Strategising to create a movement to solve the well-being issue is an opportunity to build goodwill among all lawyers. These conversations can improve optimism, trust, resilience and determination, and create positive relationships.

In a professional context, this would represent a departure from administrative staff giving CLE presentations on ethics. Instead, lawyers would roll up their sleeves to initiate change among themselves. Having lawyers within the firm take responsibility for change will promote camaraderie, better physical and mental health and greater motivation, creativity and productivity.

Hiring a consultant to mediate and coach lawyers or committees can change attitudes and perspectives, and improve communication skills between lawyers. Focusing on small improvements and seeking growth opportunities will foster a community of lawyers who focus on what is working rather than what's not working. This should be an ongoing project and not a one-and-done occurrence.

9. Unity from solutions

When a group of individuals faces a common foe, there can be good news and bad news. The good news is that they unite to oppose a common enemy. The bad news is that the enemy exists.

The common foe that some lawyers, young and old, battle is the difficulty trying to maintain mental, emotional and physical health and well-being. Lack of good health among legal professionals has escalated into a crisis, no matter the part of the world, the age, background, nationality, or ethnic background of the individual, and it is taking a toll on brilliant law students, new lawyers and even experienced practitioners.

Although many Big Law firms have pledged to do more to protect legal professionals' well-being, this is no more than a good beginning – much more needs to be done. And resolution of the crisis does not rest with the law firms and bar associations alone – each individual lawyer must bring new commitment and consciousness to their law practice.

10. Awareness

Personal experience coaching hundreds of lawyers over the years has shown that if an individual has had a troubled, neglected or traumatic childhood or adolescence, the pressure of working in the legal profession can result in re-traumatisation. Lawyers can find themselves living in a war zone inside their heads as they keep pushing themselves to be model professionals. We read about far too many lawyers who have taken their own lives as the result of unresolved issues and pressures.

Clearly, awareness of what others might have been through is key to finding solutions. After that, once an individual can get beyond the old ways of doing things, the result can be new and innovative approaches, including use of technology, and in many cases the negative effects of overwork, long hours and damage to lawyers' overall health can be avoided.

11. Education

Education is an important component if lawyers are to be aware of the prolonged effects of conflict and poor communication on health and well-being. Specifically:

- Acknowledging that the legal profession is one of the top five professions for suicides emphasises the urgent need for change.
- Lawyers should come together to educate themselves about self-help strategies, stress-relieving activities and overall well-being.
- Forming multi-generational committees or teams must be a priority. An occasional seminar or a talk at the annual meeting is not enough.

An industry-wide shift is required. And it starts with gaining an understanding of what actions each lawyer and law firm needs to take, individually and together, to make legal wellness a priority.

Anne Brafford, a prominent front-line advocate for lawyer well-being,[48] told us:

> *Concerns about lawyer well-being have been percolating for decades. But what triggered the recent wave of activity in the U.S. was a 2016 study sponsored by the American Bar Association (ABA) and the Hazelden Betty Ford Foundation of nearly 13,000 lawyers.*[49] *The study found alarming rates of problematic drinking as well as elevated symptoms of depression and anxiety. These findings created a sense of urgency and catalyzed multiple initiatives across the profession to improve well-being. Among the most significant was the founding of the National Task Force on Lawyer Well-Being and the publication of its 2017 report, The Path to Lawyer Well-Being: Practical Recommendations for Positive Change, for which I was the Editor-in-Chief and a co-author.*[50] *The report spotlighted the findings of the 2016 study and offered recommendations that encouraged stakeholders across the profession to become positive change-makers. It was important to me that we define well-being in a holistic way: Well-being is not just the absence of illness but is optimal functioning in all major areas of our lives. The vast majority of lawyers do not have a diagnosable disorder but this does not mean that they are fully well and thriving.*

The 2017 report motivated the ABA to form a temporary task force called the Presidential Working Group to Advance Well-Being in the Legal Profession. One of the Group's major projects was the Well-Being Toolkit for Lawyers and Legal Employers,[51] which I authored. The Toolkit offers practical ideas and resources for individuals and organizations. Also in 2017, I authored an ABA-published book titled Positive Professionals: Creating High-Performing, Positive Firms Through the Science of Engagement.[52] It offers practical, science-based strategies to legal employers for boosting engagement and curbing burnout.

In December 2020, the National Task Force on Lawyer Well-Being changed its name to the Institute for Well-Being in Law (IWIL) and became a 501(c)(3) non-profit. Its mission statement reflects its dedication to 'the betterment of the legal profession by focusing on a holistic approach to well-being. Through advocacy, research, education, technical and resource support, and stakeholders' partnerships, it is driven to lead a culture shift in law to establish health and well-being as core centerpieces of professional success.' An important aim of IWIL is to become the hub for innovation, information, and resources for the legal profession. A major IWIL initiative aligned with this goal is Well-Being Week in Law – an

"A consistent habit of appreciation is the strongest driver of engagement. And engagement is a powerful tool."

annual, mostly-free event that occurs the first week of May to support Mental Health Awareness Month. IWIL's first annual conference will be in January 2022. The goal of these events is to encourage action and innovation across the profession to improve well-being. Many free resources are available on the IWIL website (lawyerwellbeing.net), and this collection will continue to grow.

12. Engagement

A consistent habit of appreciation is the strongest driver of engagement. And engagement is a powerful tool.

Section heads, managing partners and management teams within the firm who genuinely appreciate the younger lawyers under their care are lifting these young lawyers up. This simple act frees these lawyers to do their best work. It energises the entire staff.

There has to be a meeting of minds to achieve win/win, and to build continued success.

Invested law firms will often conclude they have neither the time nor the inclination to delve into complex relationship issues in their firm. They will engage a strategy expert, coach, or consultant to help them bridge the gap, increase engagement and inculcate loyalty in lawyers to achieve greater retention.

13. Summary

All generations can make a joint commitment to improving well-being within their firm. Given its importance, the issue is a good place to start when building unity. Lawyers can come to the table and approach productivity and profits with a focus on their own, and their colleagues', well-being.

Meaningful work in a healthy environment is an essential foundation for a cohesive firm culture; and it goes without saying that the practice of law is meaningful work!

XIII. Generations face off over post-COVID remote work

1. Introduction

As the lockdowns slowly ended, many law firms expected all of their lawyers to return to the office. A heated inter-generational debate began, on several fronts, as to whether lawyers should be required to return to the office on a full-time basis or continue to work remotely.

Many boomers believe lawyers belong in the office. Some Gen Xers and millennials think that location doesn't matter as long as the work is completed. A majority prefer to work in a hybrid fashion, a combination of home and office working. A minority prefer only to work remotely.

We conducted a poll on LinkedIn to see where the majority of the lawyers who participated preferred to work. There were over 5,000 views, and 235 participated. The results were as follows:

- office only – 17%;
- remote only – 16%; and
- hybrid – 77%.

2. A change of heart

The following story is an example of a law firm willing to relax its office-only work requirements.

Case study: Mary Ann

'Mary Ann' was a senior partner at a large firm. The firm had several offices in the United States and had a no-remote-work policy.

The office where Mary Ann worked proved unprofitable to the firm, and they decided to shut the office down. The firm ruled that each lawyer from the office should relocate. The lawyers were given the choice of either moving to the nearest city with an office, or finding themselves other jobs.

Since Mary Ann had aging parents and had lived in their New England town her entire life, she felt she had no choice but to look for another job.

She eventually found a job but was not happy; she greatly missed her old firm, where she had worked for many years.

Then COVID-19 hit. All law firms and lawyers were forced to work remotely, including Mary Ann's former firm.

Law firms that formerly would not have permitted lawyers to work remotely had a change of heart.

Mary Ann heard that her old firm was hiring and asked about the possibility of working remotely. After much discussion, her former firm rehired her and allowed her to work 100% remotely.

These kinds of compromises have become more common post-COVID-19; law firms understand that in certain cases, adopting appropriate technology enables them to hire remote workers.

3. The great resignation

What of the trends outside the legal profession?

Tension over remote working has led to a 'great resignation' in the corporate sector, with many – primarily millennial – professionals resigning from their roles because they don't want to return to full-time in-office work.

Meantime many managers, often boomers and Gen X, are insisting on a requirement to return to full-time office work post-pandemic.

While many in the corporate sector prefer some form of hybrid working, Globe and Mail journalist Rita Trichur warns that hybrid work would cause disproportionate harm to women who would be discriminated against when it comes to promotions because they would find themselves, when working at home, out of in-office power-loops where men would be represented in more significant numbers.[53]

In other cases, Wall Street banks, including Goldman Sachs, plan to require everyone to return to the office once the pandemic runs out of steam.[54] Boeing management, having experienced remote work and becoming fans, have looked to sell their corporate headquarters.[55] And among high-tech and Silicon Valley firms, many companies are instituting remote work, hybrid work, and new in-office policies. Twitter, for example, is permitting workers to go all remote,[56] and Google is allowing a hybrid option while also utilising fully remote and all in-office workers.[57] Apple announced a return-to-office policy post-pandemic, with some employees able to request exemptions, but there has been pushback from employees.[58]

Overall, the Silicon Valley approach has been to increase the amount of remote work while also retaining a significant amount of in-office work. In some cases, Silicon Valley companies are reducing compensation for those who choose to work remotely and in less expensive locales. For example, Facebook informed employees recently that if they chose to move outside Silicon Valley, their pay would decrease based on their new, lower-cost location.[59]

"We cannot foretell the future, but we can say with certainty that the pandemic has changed forever how the law is practised."

4. Look to the future

The implications of remote work for law firms may turn out to reflect those for the corporate world. There may be mass resignations in the event firms are unwilling to adopt significant remote working policies. Indeed, law firms might face the possibility of being supplanted by firms that do go fully remote.

Firms need to adapt to the new normal and adopt remote working policies that are focused on the happiness and well-being of lawyers, employees and other professionals.

The debate is very much alive, and the question of whether office, remote or hybrid working arrangements will apply in the future remains open. We cannot foretell the future, but we can say with certainty that the pandemic has changed forever how the law is practised.

XIV. The big picture

1. Questions for the leadership

There is no one-size-fits-all for closing the gap between the generations within law firms and the legal community. Each organisation will want to assess where they are. If they are genuinely committed to change, they will want to ask themselves some difficult questions:

- How is the management of the firm taking the lead to close the generational gap within the firm?
- Has the firm established a multi-generational committee to begin the discussion to solve the problems?
- Is the firm taking an honest look at the costs of attrition? A firm needs to look at the percentage of turnover and the total cost, and to track the results after implementing change.
- Has the firm hired a consultant who is familiar with the multi-generational challenges that the firm faces?
- Has the firm invested in assessments of emotional intelligence among the leadership?
- Does the firm have the unreasonable expectation that an administrative DEI staff member can singlehandedly change the firm's culture?

2. Where to begin?

2.1 Assessment

Assessment is always the place to begin. For example, we include EQ assessments with our coaching programmes. Management must know their strengths and weaknesses. Every firm is at a different level concerning their attrition, communication between the generations and diversity.

It is unproductive to think of the problem of poor inter-generational communication as something that will go away just by putting money in the budget. A law firm's management must be willing to roll up their sleeves and participate in closing the gap between the generations. The future of the legal profession is at stake.

Commitment and action are key. Firms where the management committee is unwilling to participate will risk mediocre results. With dedication and the right strategies and action plans, law firms can be transformed, bringing harmony to the generations and resulting in lower attrition rates and increased profits.

Case study: Bill

'Bill' is an associate in a large law firm. He felt disappointed and resentful when he was instructed by the partner to whom he reported to perform work which was secretarial and clerical, not legal. Bill felt alienated and considered that the more senior lawyer had overstepped his authority and treated him disrespectfully. Bill was especially resentful given that such instructions were specifically not allowed according to firm rules – but the firm didn't enforce these rules.

A number of Bill's associate colleagues had been treated likewise, and this created a major division between junior and senior lawyers. Junior lawyers believed senior lawyers saw themselves as better. Morale was deeply – and unnecessarily – impacted.

2.2 Teamwork

Transforming the way that lawyers, young and old, communicate with each other is a game-changer.

The current 'language' used by lawyers use is based on IQ, which isn't sufficient to resolve conflicts. By bringing emotional intelligence to bear, it is possible to create an atmosphere conducive to transforming the language to solve communication barriers.

Partnership ownership models are about power. Lawyers will be inclined to listen to lawyers in authority – the partners and owners of the firm. Administrative personnel in a traditional law firm structure,

"Commitment and action are key. Firms where the management committee is unwilling to participate will risk mediocre results."

for example diversity and inclusion personnel, are in a much less powerful position – they will be unable to make lasting and structural change in the absence of support from senior partners.

But when there is abuse of power by senior management, there is loss of goodwill, as in the case study below.

Case study: Malcolm
'Malcolm' is an associate at a large law firm where junior lawyers are encouraged to participate in business development as a means by which to help build the firm's revenue. An ambitious associate, Malcolm was upset when he saw senior lawyers use their position of power to encroach upon the territory of junior lawyers when they saw it was to their advantage.

A senior lawyer was introduced to a potential client by Malcolm. The senior lawyer quickly sought to sideline Malcolm by ignoring him in a meeting with the prospective client. In the end, this did not sit well with the prospective client and as a result the firm did not win the work. The net effect of this treatment discouraged Malcolm and other junior lawyers from getting involved in business development. The senior lawyers' attitudes, by focusing on personal ambition instead of teamwork with junior lawyers, harmed firm morale and cost the firm potential clients.

One successful approach to addressing this scenario is based on the creation of teams, or 'pods'. Most firms work in silos, with attendant competition. Those who advance outshine others. Instead, try creating a pod of associates, motivated to work together. Give them a deadline, with rotating leadership. The pod should monitor the deadlines. Flexibility is key: one person, for example, shouldn't be stuck doing research.

3. Summary

Some firms are much further along the road to communication and collaboration than others. So, steps going forward will vary from firm to firm. Collaborative work culture comes from commitment to empowering everyone in the firm.

One further thought on collaboration: often, individuals in the firm are afraid to speak up for fear of being shunned, labelled or ostracised. Where this is an issue, consultants from outside the firm can be invaluable in providing mediation.

XV. Thriving in a multi-generational law firm

1. Twenty-one steps

The following steps, developed over many years of practice, can help the multi-generational law firm to thrive:

1. Develop a strategy that fits your firm's culture that will bridge the communication gap.

2. Avoid silos that cause lawyers to leave and instead create a collaborative work environment by building teams or pods.

3. Create multi-generational diversity committees and hire consultants to solve problems.

4. Build a harmonious law firm culture by holding informal gatherings outside the office to create more human-to-human relationships.

5. Review the firm's policies on remote versus in-office working (especially post-pandemic) that works for all generations in the firm and promotes productivity and balance.

6. Adapt the new, post-COVID flexible working practices.

7. Utilise committees, pods and mediation to solve communication problems.

8. Focus on solutions and stop blaming and judging others by incorporating the language of emotional intelligence.

9. Decrease turnover by recreating a practice model to motivate young lawyers through communication, community and support.

10. Address issues that have caused young lawyers to leave the firm – take measures to increase engagement between senior and junior lawyers.

11. Take the initiative – management committees must create strategies that radically reduce turnover using non-traditional methods.

12. Prepare a lawyer well-being report that includes practices to improve mental health – the management committee should actively read and review the report and participate in implementing the recommendations.

13. Build a structure that creates a uniform mentoring programme – using the pods approach, mentoring can be implemented systematically.

"Assess the demands and workloads within the firm and make adjustments for well-being. Form multi-generational committees to monitor and make adjustments to workload while incorporating well-being policies."

14. Frame a mentoring programme to ensure a structure where no lawyer is left behind.

15. Have a task force apply the Mansfield Model by including diverse representation to level the playing field for diverse lawyers and women.

16. Upgrade or create – and teach – equitable practices for more inclusive mentoring.

17. Put aside differences to create a powerful alliance where everyone wins – this will be facilitated by including EQ communication styles in meetings.

18. Encourage engagement, camaraderie and communication among associates – pods will help in this regard.

19. Rotate partner mentors to foster communication with management. Using the pod model, mentorship will be provided for most associates.

20. Assess the demands and workloads within the firm and make adjustments for well-being. Form multi-generational committees to monitor and make adjustments to workload while incorporating well-being policies.

21. Make it a priority to create a powerful alliance between all lawyers by focusing on similarities as opposed to differences. Improved communication and policies will be evident.

2. Summary

These twenty-one steps will give law firms a framework to begin bridging the communication gap, increasing productivity and reducing attrition. Obviously, you cannot do everything at once. Decide on one or more steps that your firm will commit to completing.

XVI. Conclusion

In this Special Report we have provided the tools to create more harmony, profitability and productivity in the multi-generational law practice. Effective communication is the only means by which lawyers can bridge the gap between the generations.

Management teams who are serious about bridging the generational gap must outline the strategies that they will implement, and then get to work. It is not an issue that is going to get better on its own. We highly recommend that change begins with the management team, working alongside professional development, DEI and administrative staff. Management must then stay in the loop, assist with implementing change and consider the services of a consultant who specialises in multi-generational communication solutions.

Each generation has its own viewpoints and perspectives and, as when different instruments play at once, harmony can only be achieved when there is cooperation in pursuit of a common goal.

Notes

1 See: Mike Quartararo, "Law Firms Won't Adapt Unless Clients Make Them", *Above the Law*, 10 March 2020. Available at: https://abovethelaw.com/2020/03/law-firms-wont-adapt-unless-clients-make-them/.
2 NALP Foundation and Major, Lindsey & Africa (MLA), "Keeping the Keepers IV: Mobility and Management of Associate Talent", 29 October 2020. Available at: https://f.hubspotusercontent20.net/hubfs/209075/MLA-NALP_KeepingTheKeepersIV_090120-2.pdf?__hstc=51254006.d8991a807335d3bb9c7c4dd82b0a9fe6.1627111534175.1627111534175.1627111534175.1&__hssc=51254006.1.1627111534175&__hsfp=3789933508.
3 Pamela DeNeuve, "Top 400 US Law Firms Lose $9.1 Billion Due To Turnover", LinkedIn article, 25 February 2016. Available at: www.linkedin.com/pulse/top-400-us-law-firms-loose-91-billion-turnover-pamela-deneuve-/.
4 See: Elizabeth Olson, "Law Firms Weigh Retirement Rules as Baby Boomers Keep Practicing", Bloomberg Law, 3 April 2019. Available at: https://news.bloomberglaw.com/us-law-week/law-firms-weigh-retirement-rules-as-baby-boomers-keep-practicing.
5 Dylan Jackson, "The 2020 Diversity Scorecard Shows Progress, But It's More Precarious Than Ever", *American Lawyer*, 26 May 2020. Available at: www.law.com/americanlawyer/2020/05/26/the-2020-diversity-scorecard-shows-progress-but-its-more-precarious-than-ever/.
6 Destiny Peery, Paulette Brown and Eileen Letts, "Left Out and Left Behind: The Hurdles, Hassles, and Heartaches of Achieving Long-Term Legal Careers for Women of Color", American Bar Association report, 2020. Available at: www.americanbar.org/groups/diversity/women/initiatives_awards/long-term-careers-for-women/left-out-left-behind/.
7 Roberta D Liebenberg and Stephanie A Scharf, "Walking Out The Door – The Facts, Figures, And Future Of Experienced Women Lawyers In Private Practice", ALM Legal Intelligence Compass, ABA Presidential Initiative on Achieving Long Term Careers for Women in Law and American Bar Association, 2019. Available at: www.alm.com/intelligence/wp-content/uploads/2019/11/WALKING-OUT-THE-DOOR-FINAL-AS-OF-NOV-14-2019-pm.pdf.
8 Debra Cassens Weiss, "Majority of minority female lawyers consider leaving law; ABA study explains why", *ABA Journal*, 22 June 2020. Available at: www.abajournal.com/news/article/most-minority-female-lawyers-consider-leaving-law-aba-study-explains-why.
9 Allison E Laffey and Allison Ng, "Diversity and Inclusion in the Law: Challenges and Initiatives. The legal profession remains one of the least diverse of any profession. How can we change it?", American Bar Association article, 2 May 2018. Available at: www.americanbar.org/groups/litigation/committees/jiop/articles/2018/diversity-and-inclusion-in-the-law-challenges-and-initiatives/.
10 Michael Pelly, "The top commercial threats facing law firms", *Financial Review*, 12 July 2019. Available at: www.afr.com/companies/professional-services/the-top-commercial-threats-facing-law-firms-20190710-p5262d.
11 Jaskanwal D Sara, Megha Prasad, MD, Mackram F Eleid, Ming Zhang, R Jay Widmer and Amir Lerman, "Association Between Work-Related Stress and Coronary Heart Disease: A Review of Prospective Studies Through the Job Strain, Effort-Reward Balance, and Organizational Justice Models", *J Am Heart Assoc*, 27 April 2018. Available at: www.ahajournals.org/doi/full/10.1161/jaha.117.008073.
12 Frankie Wallace, "The Impact of Generation Z On the Gaming Community", *Headstuff*, 23 April 2019. Available at: www.headstuff.org/entertainment/gaming/the-impact-of-generation-z-on-the-gaming-community/.
13 Act for Youth, "Youth Statistics: Internet & Social Media". Available at: http://actforyouth.net/adolescence/demographics/internet.cfm.
14 Marketing Charts, "Teens' Social Media Preferences Update: Drastic Changes Over the Past 3 Years", 11 June 2018. Available at: www.marketingcharts.com/demographics-and-audiences/teens-and-younger-83658.jjhlsdh.
15 As with other case studies in this Special Report, the names are pseudonyms. The studies, however, are based on real examples.
16 See: https://about.linkedin.com/.
17 NALP Foundation and Major, Lindsey & Africa (MLA), "Keeping the Keepers IV", *supra* note 2.
18 BCG, "What Causes Associates to Leave Law Firms?", blog post. Available at: www.bcgsearch.com/article/900044920/What-Causes-Associates-to-Leave-Law-Firms/.
19 The figures in the table and the paragraphs following are drawn from a number of sources, including Pamela DeNeuve, "Top 400 Law Firms Lose $9.1 Billion Due To Turnover", *supra* note 3; and Ed Pole, "The True Cost of Hiring – and Terminating – a Lawyer", LawBiz, February 2013, available at: www.lawbiz.com/true-cost-of-terminating-a-lawyer.php.
20 *Ibid.*
21 Aileen Reilly, "Are Attorneys and Marriage Compatible?", *Law Practice Today*, 15 August 2018. Available at: www.lawpracticetoday.org/article/attorneys-marriage-compatible/.
22 Dana Ackley, "Emotional Intelligence: A Practical Review Of Models, Measures, And Applications", *Consulting Psychology Journal: Practice and Research*, vol 68 no 4, 2016. Available at: www.apa.org/pubs/journals/features/cpb-cpb0000070.pdf.
23 See: Itziar Urquijo, Natalio Extremera and Garazi Azanza, "The Contribution of Emotional Intelligence to Career Success: Beyond Personality Traits", *International Journal of Environmental*

Research and Public Health, 16 December 2019, available at: www.ncbi.nlm.nih.gov/pmc/articles/PMC6926721/; and Ronda Muir, "How emotional intelligence makes you a better lawyer", American Bar Association, October 2017, available at: www.americanbar.org/news/abanews/publications/youraba/2017/october-2017/how-successful-lawyers-use-emotional-intelligence-to-their-advan/.
24 Pirical infographic, 12 December 2019. Available at: https://pirical.com/blog/2019/12/11/heres-the-uk-legal-market-in-numbers-infographic.
25 American Bar Association, "ABA Profile of the Legal Profession 2021" (demographics). Available at: www.abalegalprofile.com/demographics/.
26 *Ibid.*
27 American Bar Association, "ABA Profile of the Legal Profession 2021" (women). Available at: www.abalegalprofile.com/women/.
28 RLG, "Frozen-term watch: 'White-shoe': A term that's outlived its usefulness", *The Economist*, 3 September 2010. Available at: www.economist.com/johnson/2010/09/03/frozen-term-watch-white-shoe.
29 American Bar Association, "ABA Profile of the Legal Profession 2021", *supra* note 25.
30 Axiom Law, "Forging a New Standard for Diversity in the Legal Industry", blog post, October 2019. Available at: www.axiomlaw.com/blog/forging-a-new-standard-for-diversity-in-the-legal-industry.
31 Brenda Sapino Jeffreys, "So Slow It's 'Painful': NALP Finds Incremental Law Firm Diversity Improvements", *The American Lawyer*, 2 February 2021. Available at: www.law.com/americanlawyer/2021/02/02/so-slow-its-painful-nalp-finds-incremental-law-firm-diversity-improvements/.
32 See: "Diversity rules: A closer look at Mansfield Certification", *Fivehundred* magazine. Available at: www.legal500.com/fivehundred-magazine/diversity-and-inclusion/diversity-rules-a-closer-look-at-mansfield-certification/.
33 Diversity Lab, "2016 Women in Law Hackathon", January–June 2016. Available at: www.diversitylab.com/hackathons/.
34 See: https://ms-jd.org/about/.
35 *Ibid.*
36 See: Ellen Rosen, "Report Says Wrong Fit Can Be Costly: Business of Law", Bloomberg, 12 November 2014. Available at: www.bloomberg.com/news/articles/2014-11-12/report-says-wrong-fit-can-be-costly-business-of-law. The Bloomberg piece references Mark Levin (The Right Profile) and Bruce MacEwen (Adam Smith, Esq and JD Match), "Assessing Lawyer Traits & Finding a Fit for Success", available at: https://attorneyassessment.com/wp-content/uploads/2020/04/Attorney-Trait-Assessment-Study-Whitepaper.pdf. See also: Ed Pole, "The True Cost of Hiring – and Terminating – a Lawyer", *supra* note 19; and Pamela DeNeuve, "Top 400 US Law Firms Lose $9.1 Billion Due To Turnover", *supra* note 3.
37 LexisNexis, "Hiring partners reveal new attorney readiness for real world practice", white paper, 2015. Available at: www.lexisnexis.com/documents/pdf/20150325064926_large.pdf.
38 BCG, "What Causes Associates to Leave Law Firms?", *supra* note 18.
39 Jennifer Jordan and Michael Sorell, "Why Reverse Mentoring Works and How to Do It Right", *Harvard Business Review*, 3 October 2019. Available at: https://hbr.org/2019/10/why-reverse-mentoring-works-and-how-to-do-it-right.
40 Debra Cassens Weiss, "First-year associate pay continues to rise, despite pandemic, NALP survey says", *ABA Journal*, 14 April 2021. Available at: www.abajournal.com/news/article/first-year-associate-pay-continues-to-rise-despite-pandemic-nalp-survey-says.
41 See: National Task Force on Lawyer Well Being (now the Institute for Well-Being in Law), "The Path to Lawyer Well-Being: Practical Recommendations for Positive Change", November 2017. Available at:
www.americanbar.org/groups/professional_responsibility/task_force_lawyer_wellbeing/.
42 World Health Organization, *Promoting Mental Health: concepts, emerging evidence, practice*, WHO, 2004.
43 Constitution of the World Health Organization. Available at: www.who.int/about/governance/constitution.
44 Kira M Newman, "How Much of Your Happiness Is Under Your Control?", *Greater Good Magazine*, 18 February 2020. Available at: https://greatergood.berkeley.edu/article/item/how_much_of_your_happiness_is_under_your_control.
45 Brian Cuban, *The Addicted Lawyer: Tales of the Bar, Booze, Blow, and Redemption*, Post Hill Press, 2017. The quote that follows was made directly to the authors.
46 National Task Force on Lawyer Well-Being, "The Path to Lawyer Well-Being", *supra* note 41. Pamela DeNeuve, co-author of this Special Report, was honoured to be a peer reviewer of the report. The report refers, for the statistics quoted in Table 10, to PR Krill, R Johnson and L Albert, "The Prevalence of Substance Abuse and other Mental Health Concerns Among American Attorneys", *Journal of Addiction Medicine*, vol 10 no 1, January/February 2016. Available at: https://journals.lww.com/journaladdictionmedicine/fulltext/2016/02000/the_prevalence_of_substance_use_and_other_mental.8.aspx.
47 *Ibid.*
48 Anne Brafford is owner of Aspire, whose aim is to "help law firms and lawyers grow and thrive together by building engaging work cultures". See: https://aspire.legal/.
49 James Podgers, "Younger lawyers are most at risk for substance abuse and mental health

problems, a new study reports", *ABA Journal*, 7 February 2016. Available at: www.abajournal.com/news/article/younger_lawyers_are_most_at_risk_for_substance_abuse_and_mental_health_prob.
50 National Task Force on Lawyer Well-Being, "The Path to Lawyer Well-Being", *supra* note 41.
51 Ann M Brafford, *Well-being Toolkit for Lawyers and Legal Employers*, American Bar Association, 2017. Available at: www.americanbar.org/content/dam/aba/administrative/lawyer_assistance/ls_colap_well-being_toolkit_for_lawyers_legal_employers.pdf.
52 Anne M Brafford, *Positive Professionals: Creating High-Performing Profitable Firms Through the Science of Engagement*, American Bar Association, 2017.
53 Rita Trichur, "Hybrid work risks becoming the next 'career killer' for women", *The Globe and Mail*, 1 September 2021. Available at: www.theglobeandmail.com/business/article-hybrid-work-risks-becoming-the-next-career-killer-for-women/.
54 Jack Kelly, "Wall Street Banks that Demanded Workers to Return to Their Offices May Have to Change Their Plans Due to Delta Variant", *Forbes*, 4 August 2021. Available at: www.forbes.com/sites/jackkelly/2021/08/04/wall-street-banks-that-demanded-workers-to-return-to-their-offices-may-have-to-change-their-plans-due-to-delta-variant/?sh=5c1e2afe7356.
55 Dominic Gates and Katherine Anne Long, "Boeing eyes sale of commercial airplanes HQ, considers mobile CEO and rethinks office work", *The Seattle Times*, 16 October 2020. Available at: www.seattletimes.com/business/boeing-aerospace/boeing-eyes-sale-of-seattle-area-commercial-airplanes-complex-considers-mobile-work-by-everyone-up-to-the-ceo/.
56 Kari Paul, "Twitter announces employees will be allowed to work from home 'forever'", *The Guardian*, 12 May 2020. Available at: www.theguardian.com/technology/2020/may/12/twitter-coronavirus-covid19-work-from-home.
57 Jack Kelly, "Google Announces A Hybrid Return-To-Work Plan, Including Both Remote And In-Office Options", *Forbes*, 6 May 2021. Available at: www.forbes.com/sites/jackkelly/2021/05/06/google-announces-a-hybrid——return-to-work-plan-including-both-remote-and-in-office-options/?sh=412da2da3831.
58 Zoe Schiffer, "Apple employees push back against returning to the office in internal letter", *The Verge*, 4 June 2021. Available at: www.theverge.com/2021/6/4/22491629/apple-employees-push-back-return-office-internal-letter-tim-cook.
59 Michael Liedtke and Barbara Ortutay, "'You Can't Put the Genie Back in the Bottle.' Silicon Valley Struggles to Transition Out of Remote Work", *Time*, 8 September 2021. Available at: https://time.com/6095907/silicon-valley-remote-work/.

About the authors

Pamela DeNeuve
Lawyer and law firm strategist, DeNeuve & Associates
pamela@pameladeneuve.com

Pamela DeNeuve began consulting and coaching lawyers in Los Angeles in 1992. She helped AM100 law firms expand their practices by negotiating multi-million-dollar deals. In 2005 she created a consulting business serving firms in Hong Kong and Shanghai.

Pamela served as a peer reviewer for the groundbreaking National Task Force on Lawyer Well-Being's *Creating a Movement to Improve Well-Being in the Legal Profession*, published in 2017 by the American Bar Association.

Pamela helps lawyers scale and grow their practices to increase profits and productivity while escalating engagement and communication. Her clients have included lawyers from the silent generation, baby boomers, Gen Xers, millennials and Gen Z.

Pamela previously hosted a weekly programme, "Lawyer of the Week," interviewing peak-performing lawyers internationally. She speaks to bar associations and conferences worldwide.

She is a contributor to *HuffPost* and *Medium* and continues to write extensively about multi-generational challenges and lawyer well-being.

John Grimley
Writer and editor
john@johngrimley.com

John Grimley specialises in writing and publishing services for the legal services sector internationally. He is editor and publisher of Asia Law Portal, focused on the business of law in the Asia-Pacific region. In

2014 he authored *A Comprehensive Guide to the Asia-Pacific Legal Markets*, published by Ark Group.

John has helped law firms articulate their unique value propositions in international markets for over 20 years. Most notably he established and directed an EU-focused business development initiative for AmLaw 100 firm Patton Boggs LLP, focused on foreign sovereign governments, multinational corporations and investment funds.

At the inception of his career, he served as a writer to US President George HW Bush in the White House. An American lawyer licensed in the District of Columbia for more than 25 years, he holds a Juris Doctor degree from the University of San Diego School of Law.

About Globe Law and Business

Globe Law and Business was established in 2005. From the very beginning, we set out to create law books which are sufficiently high level to be of real use to the experienced professional, yet still accessible and easy to navigate. Most of our authors are drawn from Magic Circle and other top commercial firms, both in the UK and internationally.

Our titles are carefully produced, with the utmost attention paid to editorial, design and production processes. We hope this results in high-quality publications that are easy to read, and a pleasure to own. Our titles are also available as ebooks, which are compatible with most desktop, laptop and tablet devices. In 2018 we expanded our portfolio to include journals and Special Reports, available both digitally and in hard copy format, and produced to the same high standards as our books.

In the spring of 2021, we were very pleased to announce the start of a new chapter for Globe Law and Business following the acquisition of law books under the imprint Ark Publishing. We are very much looking forward to working with our new Ark authors, many of whom are well known to us, and to further developing the law firm management list, among other areas.

We'd very much like to hear from you with your thoughts and ideas for improving what we offer. Please do feel free to email me at sian@globelawandbusiness.com with your views.

Sian O'Neill
Managing director
Globe Law and Business
www.globelawandbusiness.com